How to
Stage
Greek
Tragedy
Today

How to Stage Greek Tragedy Today

Simon Goldhill

The University of Chicago Press
Chicago and London

SIMON GOLDHILL is professor of Greek at
Cambridge University.

The University of Chicago Press, Chicago 60637
The University of Chicago Press,
Ltd., London
© 2007 by Simon Goldhill
All rights reserved. Published 2007
Printed in the United States of America

16 15 14 13 12 11 10 09 08 07
1 2 3 4 5

ISBN-13: 978-0-226-30127-3 (cloth)
ISBN-13: 978-0-226-30128-0 (paper)
ISBN-10: 0-226-30127-3 (cloth)
ISBN-10: 0-226-30128-1 (paper)

Library of Congress
Cataloging-in-Publication Data
Goldhill, Simon.
  How to stage Greek tragedy today / Simon
Goldhill.
    p. cm.
  Includes bibliographical references and index.
  ISBN-13: 978-0-226-30127-3 (cloth : alk. paper)
  ISBN-10: 0-226-30127-3 (cloth : alk. paper)
  ISBN-13: 978-0-226-30128-0 (pbk. : alk. paper)
  ISBN-10: 0-226-30128-1 (pbk. : alk. paper)
  1. Greek drama (Tragedy) 2. Greek drama—
Presentation, Modern. I. Title.
  PA3238.G65 2007
  882'.0109—dc22

                                    2007018626

♾ The paper used in this publication meets the
minimum requirements
of the American National Standard for
Information Sciences—Permanence
of Paper for Printed Library Materials, ANSI
Z39.48-1992.

Contents

Introduction

The genesis of this book is a simple enough story. In my capacity as producer of the Cambridge Greek Play in 2004 I had run a conference in Cambridge on "tragedy in performance," at which Corin Redgrave, then playing King Lear for the Royal Shakespeare Company at Stratford, had spoken. A few weeks later, he phoned me in my office and asked if I could recommend some reading for his sister, Vanessa, who was preparing to play Hecuba in London. I hummed and hawed, and promised to send him a few suggestions. But it became clear to me that it was actually rather difficult to recommend a book or even an article that would suit the bill. I had my standard academic bibliography, of course. Euripides and *Hecuba* in particular have been discussed by scholars with real insight and flair. It would be easy enough to suggest a couple of chapters that would let an actor or director see where the current state of literary critical argument is.[1] But that did not seem to be what was really required. There are also some fascinating discussions of how ancient Greek plays might have been staged in fifth-century Athens, and of the politics of Greek drama.[2] But again, this did not seem to go to the heart of the issue. When I visited Vanessa Redgrave in the theater during the troubled run of *Hecuba*, she was (still) reading my book *Reading Greek Tragedy*, and it became all too clear to me that such an introduction—literary, argumentative, historical—could not answer her particular needs (because it did not address them). What was wanted was a book that looked at the problems of producing Greek tragedy from the perspective of a modern company. So I decided to write it—and here it is.

The background to this book is the extraordinary explosion of performances of Greek tragedy in contemporary theater. In the last thirty years, every major capital of the world has had serious and frequent productions of ancient tragedies, and in the case of London, New York, Paris, and Berlin in particular there have been a quite remarkable number of often hugely successful performances. Such professional interest is matched by the college campus, where literally hundreds of performances are advertised every year. This revival shows no sign of slowing down. *How to Stage Greek Tragedy Today* is self-consciously part of this phenomenon, and its agenda is to help companies see what is at stake in producing a Greek tragedy now, as well as helping them to produce the best possible performance.

The book highlights what I regard as the six most pressing problems that face any company that chooses to produce a Greek tragedy. Each of the six chapters takes one of these basic and foundational issues, and, in each case, looks first at whether we can learn anything from the ancient world, and then discusses how modern companies have tried to solve these difficulties in the theater, and analyzes their successes and failures. Theater as a living medium needs constantly to reinvent itself—to continue to explore ancient genres and modern techniques. So it seems to me to be wholly counter-

productive to try to lay down the law about how Greek tragedy *must* be produced. Rather, in this book I see my task as
to define as clearly as possible why the ancient plays are so
hard to produce well—since recognizing exactly what a problem is, is halfway to finding a solution; lessons from great
productions or flawed productions show how a performance
can soar or flounder. This approach is designed to help directors and actors see as sharply as possible the pitfalls and
mountains in front of them—to stimulate the imagination,
rather than laying out my fantasy of how I would direct my
favorite tragedies. Because my approach is problem-based, no
single performance or tragedy is treated to a full and exhaus-
tive analysis.

So what are these six big questions? The first is theatrical space. Greek plays were written for a particular style of
amphitheater: what are the implications of this for modern
productions and how do the physical resources of modern
theaters respond to this challenge? The second is the chorus. Every Greek tragedy has a chorus, and few modern productions know what to do with this group of people singing
lyric songs about ancient myths and morality. The third is the
role of the actor: what are the specific difficulties that these
strange, ancient scripts with their formal language and long
set speeches provide for a modern trained performer? The
fourth is politics. Tragedy is an inherently political genre, and
plays like *Antigone* or the *Oresteia* have repeatedly been staged
to make a political point in the modern world. But how can
plays of the fifth century BC talk to us today? Why do some
performances of ancient tragedy seem to have an immense
political impact in our contemporary theater and others seem
merely strained and modish? The fifth area is translation. If
all translators are traitors, as the Italian proverb puts it, what
are the implications of choosing a particular script—and how
should such a choice be made? Sixth and finally, Greek plays
regularly bring onstage not only larger-than-life heroes and

the most beautiful woman ever, but also a whole cast of divinities. How on earth can modern theater deal with these figures from ancient myth and religion? These six big questions need integrated, thought-through, and theatrically powerful answers—or any production is heading for disaster.

]]] [[[

It should be clear from the outset that this book is not a history of the multiform performances of Greek tragedy over the last hundred years. There have been several wonderful contributions in recent years to what is becoming a burgeoning field ("reception studies"), and I have learnt from them.[3] But almost every production discussed in this book I have seen myself in the theater, and the few others I have seen on video.[4] I have made no attempt whatsoever to cover the full range of productions of even a single Greek tragedy in one country: my examples are chosen because they have been widely seen by contemporary audiences, and because they exemplify the major problems I am concerned with. They also represent some of the greatest directors and performers of our era engaging with Greek tragedy.

Nor is this a handbook for directors or actors: there are no acting exercises, no advice on how to deal with theater management, no suggestions on size of cast, cost of scenery, and so forth, though all of these are crucially involved in moving from an idea to a performance in a theater. Nor is it a study of how ancient plays were performed in the ancient world: my interest here is not in such history but in contemporary theater. The ancient world will again and again reveal essential insights, but those who want the full details of fifth-century Athenian theater will have to go elsewhere.

This book is aimed at anyone involved with contemporary theater and with Greek tragedy. I have deliberately restricted the footnotes, in what feels like a brutal manner to a professional classicist (and limited the bibliography to works in English). Many academic friends will recognize where I have learnt from their work, some of which appears in the further reading. I hope everyone will recognize that for a book such as this the benefits of smooth reading outweigh the duty of acknowledging every debt.

The project stems, however, first and foremost from years of sitting enthralled in theaters—often with despair and regret, sometimes with amazement and awe. I have been lucky enough to talk to and listen to many great actors and directors and translators speaking about their work with ancient theater. I have also had the extraordinary privilege of participating closely in three productions of the Cambridge Greek Play, on each occasion with a wonderful professional team of directors, designers, and composers. Jane Montgomery and especially Annie Castledine have shown me a great deal about how theater is made: above all, they have given me a constantly insightful perspective on what questions these strange and wonderful scripts, true pinnacles of the theatrical repertoire, present to a director or an actor. Helene Foley has been an inspiring guide to the American theatrical scene, and, as ever, Froma Zeitlin my companion in thought. Over the years, Oliver Taplin, Pat Easterling, Edith Hall, and Fiona Macintosh have taught me much more than I might have let on at first blush. Helen Morales advised cannily as the book took shape, as did Annie Castledine. Brigid Larmour, producer, director, and general all-round star, read it all, and gave crucial advice and encouragement. The book is dedicated to her, for all thirty years of dramatic exchanges.

Chapter One
Space and Concept

First, Find Your Space . . .

A theatrical event cannot happen without a theatrical space. This can be as formal and grand as the Metropolitan Opera House in New York or as simple and spontaneous as a street actor's power to create her own "vasty fields of France" with a gesture. The relation between performance and its space is integral to any form of drama.

When there are so many shapes of theater, such differences in physical and financial resources between companies, and so many plays and directors, is there anything general that can usefully be said about dramatic space and Greek tragedy? Does the spatial organization of ancient theater matter at all for a modern production? The answer to both of these questions is simply "yes." Greek tragedy was originally written for a particular style of theatrical space. This space is fully built into the writing of Greek plays. The internal dynamics of each play will be lost in performance if the logic of this spatial organization is ignored. Understanding the principles of ancient dramatic space is essential for a successful modern production of these scripts.

The Problem: Ancient Theater and Modern Spaces

The standard image of ancient theater is familiar from the tourist brochures of Greece: the huge amphitheater, with steeply raked wedges of seating around a circular dance floor (and great acoustics, which the guides always demonstrate by dropping a coin, which can be heard in the back row). This circular dance floor is called the *orchestra*, and the chorus performed its songs and dances on it. Opposite the audience, at the far end of the orchestra, there was a low stage in front of the *skene*, a stage building with a prominent central door (fig. 1). The individual actors (as opposed to the chorus) performed primarily on the stage. The stage building could

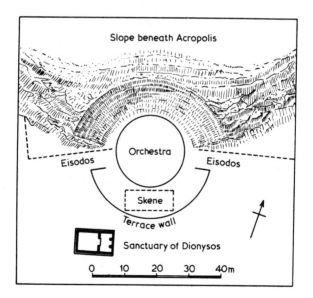

1 A schematic plan of the theater of Dionysus in Athens.

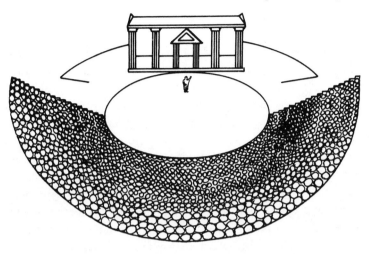

2 A sense of the acting space of the theater of Dionysus in Athens.

be used to represent a palace, a cave, a hut, a tent—any inside space. From the time of late Aeschylus at least, a rolling platform (*ekkuklema*) could bring a tableau from inside the building to the stage. Above the building was a walkway, which could be used for the entrance of the gods, high above the human sphere. But it could also be used for humans for scenes enacted on a roof or on city walls. There was also a crane, which could fly in characters above the roof. This may have been how gods made their appearance at the end of plays (the *deus ex machina*, "god from the machine"); it was certainly mobilized for flying scenes. There were two long entrance walkways on either side of the arena, along which characters, including the chorus, entered and exited the performance space (fig. 2).

This simple description conceals generations of scholarly argument, and there is nothing to suggest that all the problems are likely to be solved to everyone's satisfaction in the near future.[1] But for a modern company approaching a Greek tragedy this description is enough to provide a set of essential coordinates—and to reveal a host of fundamental implications for performance.

First, the stage is defined over and against the dancing area of the orchestra. This dynamic between stage and orchestra is central to the actors' choreography. The chorus's circular dances, rather than any necessary physical boundary, define the dance area as a charged arena. The center of this circle is bound to attract a particularly powerful focus—and there is no reason why the actors as well as the chorus members cannot make it their own; but articulating the sides of the circle is essential for creating the bounded space and for the dynamics of representation within it. Second, there is for Greek tragedy a powerful focus on the central door of the stage building as the defining boundary of a stage area. We will see shortly the varied and powerful ways the dramatists worked with this focus, but it remains a basic element of the theatrical space. Third, the entrance walkways expand the focus of attention outward, and provide a long passage for the transitions from stage to offstage. Fourth, the height of the stage and, especially, the stage building itself create a vertical axis. These four elements—the stage in relation to the orchestra, the door, the rampways, the roof—provide the spatial matrix in which tragedy is enacted. Although each play uses these varied resources in a different way, any modern performance has to respond to this organization of space.

Now this description of Greek theatrical space has been deliberately put in the most general terms. But such a description is enough to show immediately some of the problems faced by a modern production. The proscenium arch, a standard stage organization in traditional modern theaters, can easily provide for an excellent central doorway, but with the usual positioning of an audience, the square frame of the proscenium offers little sense of an orchestra, that is, any space that makes sense of the chorus's role. The entrances in modern theaters are usually the short wing area, which restrict the long entrances and exits so often utilized by the Greek dramatists. Theater in the round, on the other hand, which is common in smaller modern theaters, can create wonderful spaces for choral performance. The circular floor, ringed by the audience, seems perfect for the collective dance. But this type of spatial organization usually fails to provide a central door with a strong enough focus, or a contrast between actor's space and choral space. Both with a proscenium arch and with theater in the round, the different heights of the stage and the building roof—the vertical axis—are also all too often lost in modern production.

For a modern company to try somehow to reproduce the shape or design of ancient theater would be a fool's errand: the conditions of antiquity are lost to us. Nor should a modern production aim for archaeological accuracy (the first Victorian productions of Greek drama were really proud of their truthfulness to ancient costume and artifact: they look hilariously clunky to modern eyes, full of false beards and men in sheets). Rather, the aim of a modern production should be to create a theatrical space that can recognize and work with the way that Greek tragedy has been written—a space that minimizes the dire effects of trying to force a round play into a square box. Let us look first at how four modern productions have found their solutions to this problem—which inevitably reflect different financial and physical resources as well as different imaginative responses to the staging of Greek tragedy.

Working with the Problem of Space

Ariane Mnouchkine directed *Les Atrides,* her version of Aeschylus's *Oresteia* and Euripides' *Iphigeneia at Aulis,* in Paris in the 1990s.[2] It traveled to England (where I first saw it), to New York, and to various other cities in countries across the world (France, Germany, Italy, Canada): it was seen not just by appreciative theater audiences but also by many of the best directors and actors in contemporary theater (and its influence was immediately apparent in other productions). Here, I want just to recall the set, and how the work of the designer and director responded to the problems I have just outlined. Mnouchkine in each city took a large, barnlike space in which the set was developed by the designer, Guy-Claude François. (The performance in England took place at Bradford, an industrial town in the north, in part because of the need for exactly the right sort of space to accommodate the demands of the set. In New York, it was in the Park Slope Armory, which is not even close to off-off Broadway.) In the Parisian theater, the foyer of the theater was decorated with a huge map of the Mediterranean showing Agamemnon's journey, and books and photos about Greek life and Greek food were for sale. (Katie Mitchell's superb *Phoenissae* at the Royal Shakespeare Company in Stratford, England, brought Greece into the mind rather more sensuously—if with a touch of the fey—by giving each member of the audience a sprig of thyme or mint when they entered, and the smell of the theater was immediately redolent of a Greek mountainside.) The audience were funneled through toward the acting space past what looked like an archaeological dig, with terra-cotta statues in shallow trenches. When the chorus appeared onstage, it was as if these statues came to sudden and exuberant life—a thrilling coup de théâtre. (Unfortunately, in Bradford and in the United States, these statues and the trenches could not be used.) The audience sat in large, steep bleachers, a simple scaffolded construction with very basic seats. Underneath this structure, the cast changed, did their makeup, and prepared, in full view of the audience as they entered the theater to take up their seats. The stage space itself was a large rectangular floor, surrounded by a wall, about the height of a person. This wall was like the wall of a bullfighting ring, in that actors could flee behind it in places through a screening fore-wall, or leap up toward its height, or appear behind it (fig. 3). On one side of

3 The set of Mnouchkine's *Les Atrides*, during a rehearsal. The large central doors facing the audience rise above and behind the smaller doors in the wall, behind, round, and on which the actors leapt, hid, and watched the action. The musical instruments can be seen on the right of the picture.

this space (stage left), on another scaffolded platform, was the musician who had an impressive battery of oriental percussive instruments. The chorus entered through huge double doors opposite the audience, but the protagonists entered and exited through an opening in the seating of the audience, an opening which represented the door to the palace.

This deceptively simple design was utilized brilliantly by the production, which placed a great deal of emphasis on music and dance. The exceptionally large stage provided a wonderful canvas for some stirring choral dancing: the production had immense energy, driven forward by the pulsating rhythms of the music. The visibility of the musician and the excitement of his playing were absolutely integral to the performance. The stage was large enough for a full-scale chorus to move with brilliant vibrancy, in complex, sweeping, collective patterns. This space was especially well suited to the

Oresteia. The trilogy, first of all, has an enormous role for the chorus. The odes are some of the longest and most dense in all of Greek tragedy, and the chorus plays a particularly active role in the plot, especially in the *Eumenides*, where the chorus of Furies chase and finally prosecute Orestes in court in Athens. The set was designed to showcase the collective movement and words of the chorus.

What is more, the *Oresteia* is obsessed with the construction of a sense of a social collective. It starts with the problems of one royal household but ends in the city of Athens with a torch-lit procession of women to the Acropolis to sacrifice to the gods. It debates and celebrates what social justice can mean, and it promotes the order of the city as the necessary if flawed framework for a proper life for humans. The integration of the chorus of Furies into the city becomes the potent symbol of the potential of the city, as a place where conflict can be controlled by the institutions of social order. Mnouchkine's focus on the chorus made sure that the democratic ideal of the collective remained central to Aeschylus's masterpiece.

Every production of the *Oresteia* has to engage with the play's gripping politics, and Mnouchkine's left-wing feminist sympathies were clear especially in the final play of the trilogy (translated for this production by the famous French thinker Hélène Cixous, the latest in a long history of trenchant feminist engagement with this trilogy).[3] Even when the politics of her vision grated, as with the representation of the Furies as a pair of bag ladies with a pack of wild dog/apes, the stage set was constantly worked to keep the *collective* of the chorus central to the trilogy, as a political idea as well as a physical group. The set of *Les Atrides* was perfectly designed to give the chorus maximum expressive scope.

The set was also splendidly managed by the individual actors, however. At one level, an intense focus for moments of storytelling was created by an actor at the very center of

the stage: these passages of storytelling were often delivered with a deep physical stillness, encircled by the chorus as an audience onstage. This creation of an arena for the protagonists was fundamental for the scenes of conflict, enacted as if ringed by the walls of the set and the bodily encirclement of the chorus. At another level, Apollo's athletic power and speed around the large stage (and its walls) gave a quite astounding sense of a god in flight—and of the airiness and scope of the stage. This is especially important as the trilogy opens out in the third play from the tormented household to the widest political frame. The *scale* of the stage itself, reminiscent of the vastness of the ancient Greek arenas, became a marvelous resource, now to form a pocket of still intensity within its expanse, now to explode into flashing movement.

Les Atrides was a thrilling production, which influenced many companies over the next ten years. Its set was designed with the company and its values closely in mind, and it was an integral part of the play's success. Yet the design also made one choice which quite changed the dynamics of the *Oresteia*'s staging. The set placed the central door (as it were) in the central block of audience seating, so that characters went in and out of the house of Atreus by returning to the changing area beneath the bleachers.

This central door is perhaps the most charged space in the *Agamemnon* and *Libation Bearers*. The most famous scene of the *Agamemnon* is the "carpet scene," where Clytemnestra spreads costly purple tapestries on the floor in front of her husband Agamemnon, returned now after ten years away at the Trojan war; she demands that he enter the house across this swathe of blood-colored cloth, and despite his deep reluctance to trample on such finery, he is persuaded to step from his chariot onto the rugs. It is a moment which symbolically seals his death, as he both gives up his power to a woman, and treads a blood-colored path toward the inside of his own house. Clytemnestra here controls the access to the door of

the palace. She has appeared at the door for each scene of the drama, to assert her authority and demonstrate her control. No one comes in or out of the palace without her say. The inside of the palace becomes uncannily charged as a place where horrors occur, and, typically for the gender politics of this piece, a place where the corrupt female now holds sway. Cassandra, the prophetess, describes the inside of the palace in the most vivid and dismaying terms as "god-hated, complicit, a charnel-house, flowing with human blood." It is a hidden space, where dark curses, terrible desires, and transgressive acts lurk. The door marks the divide between the world of the stage and the recesses of the house. Clytemnestra comes out of the house with the bodies of her murdered husband and Cassandra on the ekkuklema, to display—and revel in—the violence committed within.

When Orestes comes back to kill his mother, the moment of knocking on the door is the first irrevocable step of revenge. He calls for the ruler to come out, and adds that a man would be most seemly. But instead of Aegisthus, Clytemnestra's lover, it is Clytemnestra herself who again appears at the door, now to welcome in her future murderer and unrecognized son. Like his father, Orestes enters the palace with Clytemnestra. But Orestes in his turn will appear on the ekkuklema over the bodies of his slaughtered mother and the cowardly Aegisthus. Who controls the boundary of the house is a fundamental issue for the gender politics of this play: the door is the scene where such conflicts are acted out. This is a great example of how the ancient dramatists could isolate one aspect of the stage, objectify it, and fill it with immense significance over the running of the play.

The decision of Mnouchkine and François to put the palace door in the audience seating inverted this dynamic of movement. No longer does the king progress away from the audience toward his death, no longer does the door stare at the audience throughout the action. What was gained by such

a startling decision, apart from the practical benefit of having the characters leave directly toward the changing area? The audience could now see the face of Agamemnon or of Orestes as he progressed toward the awful, hidden space—which was undoubtedly a deeply affecting angle of vision on the scene. More reflective members of the audience might have considered that the horror behind the locked door was now located within themselves as a body (as it were)—a point which gains poignant force from Cixous's feminist argument about the inevitable absorption of misogynist myth inside the psyche of the subjects of a patriarchal system: we are all victims of the horrific fantasies of male violence.

But it seems to me that in dramatic terms more was lost than was gained. The door was no longer there to be seen: the visible barrier, hiding such miseries, no longer brooded over the stage; Clytemnestra could not appear before the audience's gaze to block the way of the returning king; Orestes could not walk away from the support of the chorus, away from the audience, toward the frightening and silent doorway. Clytemnestra or Orestes could not come out of the house toward the audience with the bloody evidence of their acts. To my mind, for all that I could make an intellectual case for the shift in the theatrical dynamic, the power of Aeschylus's dramaturgy had been undervalued.

]]] [[[

My second example, Lee Breuer's production of *Gospel at Colonus* [1985] in New York, a gospel version of Sophocles' *Oedipus at Colonus* (with bits of *Antigone* added), took a diametrically opposed approach to Mnouchkine's *Oresteia*.[4] The theatrical space was small, crowded, and intense, with almost no scope for the sweep and drive of a chorus's dancing (though every performance I saw ended up with the audience on their feet and dancing). This too was a hugely successful production, revived twenty years later on Broadway. (As so often, what starts as radical, innovatory, and marginal ends up right in the middle of the mainstream.) It reveals a quite different conceptualization of the theatrical arena for tragedy.

The *Gospel at Colonus* also used steeply raked seating for the audience, and used these banks of seating to create a circular arena. But one of the banks of seats was wholly taken up with a gospel choir, mainly of female singers, dressed in brightly colored African robes: the chorus (fig. 8, p. 57). These choir members could stand to sing, and fan their hands, but otherwise did not move at all. There was no dancing by the chorus here. One interpretation of the Greek chorus, as we will see in the next chapter, is that the chorus mediates and directs the audience reaction to the tragic events onstage. In this set for the *Gospel at Colonus*, the chorus is literally in the position of the audience: they share seating with the spectators. What's more, with their typically engaged gospel cries of encouragement, or agreement or reaction to the story unfolding before them, the choir often did precisely direct and manage the audience's response. Onstage was a white piano, where Oedipus sat, which dominated the acting space. There was a small electric band by the side of the stage led by a guitarist conductor. The choir also had an exuberant director who leapt and conducted with extravagant gestures. A reading lectern for the preacher was prominently placed. The space for the actors on this set was as restricted as the space in *Les Atrides* was expansive. The performance was more like a gospel service, with preacher, choir, and congregation, and the dramatic interaction was constantly mediated through the formal restraints of such a service.

Yet this simple set had one particular feature that worked especially well—and which again shows how an attentiveness to the resources of Greek theater and the specifics of the one play is essential for a successful modern staging. The characters each entered down a long stairway from the top of the raked seating, between the chorus and the audience. An entrance or exit could take several minutes, and was in direct contact with the chorus and audience all the way down or up. Why was this so important and so effective?

Oedipus at Colonus tells the story of the aged Oedipus at the end of his life. Blind, in beggar's rags, he is wandering through Greece led by his daughter Antigone. When he reaches Colonus, and the Grove of the Furies, he recognizes that he has reached the place where it is fated for him to die, and to be transformed from his mortal status. He is to become a spirit (a *heros*, or "hero" in English), and after his death and transformation, he will protect the land where his body is lain to rest. There actually was a cult of Oedipus at Colonus, a place in the territory of Athens, a couple of miles from the city, and when the Athenians fought a battle there against the invading Thebans and defeated them, it was said that the figure of Oedipus had appeared in order to support the Athenians. During the play, Oedipus sits in the Grove of the Furies to await his end. He is visited by his other faithful daughter, Ismene, who brings him news of Thebes: his sons and Creon know of the oracle which predicts the benefits Oedipus will bring to the land where he is buried, and Creon is on his way to try to persuade Oedipus to return to Thebes. Theseus, the king of Athens, then arrives, and formally accepts Oedipus into Athens, and promises him support and succor. Then Creon indeed arrives from Thebes, and begs Oedipus to forget his former banishment and to come home. When Oedipus refuses, Creon no longer begs but threatens: he has captured Ismene and is happy to use her as a bargaining counter. Oedipus calls on his new protector Theseus, who duly forces Creon to release the young woman. Oedipus's son Polyneices then arrives to ask for his father's support in his campaign to capture the throne of Thebes from his brother, Eteocles. Oedipus sends him away with a curse, which will eventually result in the fratricidal killing of both young men.

Finally Oedipus himself leaves with Theseus to meet his mysterious end.

This brief and oversimplified retelling of the complicated plot of Sophocles' final play emphasizes that it is a drama structured around journeys and arrivals. Oedipus and Antigone arrive, wandering, and enter the Grove of the Furies. As Oedipus is seated on a rock, he is visited in turn by his daughter, by Theseus, by Creon, and by Polyneices. When Oedipus leaves the rock, it is to progress to his death. There is in this play no focus at all on any central door. There is no "inside" space. Rather, the play is centered on the rock in the middle of the grove. Because of this dramatic structure, the long entrance stairway of the set of the *Gospel at Colonus* proved a brilliant part of the design. Each major character could come slowly down the long stairway, to be recognized by the chorus or by the speakers onstage. The entrances became instantiations of the journey toward and away from the blind Oedipus, at the heart of the stage at the piano. The journey of Oedipus himself became embodied in his progress down the stairs and then away toward his mysterious transformation. The long, flat entrance ramps of the Greek theater found a striking modern version in the steep stairway of *Gospel at Colonus*. This stage set was perfectly designed for this—and only this—tragedy.

]]] [[[

Every Greek play was originally written for staging within the resources of ancient theater. When this basic structure of the drama is ignored, the effect can be disastrous. Euripides' *Medea* is a perfect example. It is, first of all, essential for this play that there is a strong sense of the inside space of the house and outside space of the public sphere. The play opens with Medea screaming inside the house, and the nurse and then the tutor outside worrying about her terrifying emotional outbursts. The inside of the house is instantly imaged as the inhabitation of a wild and disturbed feminine force. When Medea comes out, however, it is to offer a calm, funny, manipulative speech to the chorus, whose help she needs. "I have come out of the house, women of Corinth," she says as she enters the arena of the stage, "so that you should not blame me." In this outside space, Medea tricks, deceives, and argues with the men who want to thwart her. We watch her rhetoric at work with grim fascination. But when she takes her children back inside the house, it is terrifying. We know that behind these locked doors terrible things are about to happen.

In Deborah Warner's production in London (2001), which transferred from Dublin and went on to New York—starring Fiona Shaw and Jonathan Cake—this sense of the inside and the outside was extremely well articulated in Tom Pye's design.[5] The wall of the house filled the back of the set, and in front of the wall was a glass screen with its own door. Medea could appear between the wall and the glass, and the effect of her entrance, dragging her dead children's bodies and smearing the glass with their blood was deeply shocking. The glass screen was a brilliant metaphor for the problem Medea poses the other characters and the audience. Can we see through her rhetoric? Do we know what she really wants? How do we view the household she has made with Jason? The glass that lets us see the house becomes the very medium on which the horror of the murder is scrawled.

But the end of *Medea* poses a different set of problems. In Euripides' play Medea appears above the house carrying the bodies of her children on a chariot drawn by dragons, a chariot sent for her by her grandfather, the Sun god, Helios. This was almost certainly a moment for the crane, and a stunning dramatic spectacle, which caught the imagination of later artists (fig. 4). Medea cannot be touched by Jason, whom she has humiliated and destroyed emotionally. Below her, he begs vainly for the bodies of his children to bury, and

4 A wine bowl from around 400 BC with a picture of Medea rising in her dragon chariot, framed by the sun, as befits a descendent of the Sun God. The murdered children are draped over the altar beneath, flanked by distraught mourners.

curses vainly his barbarian wife. She is in the position of the deus ex machina, the god from the machine. When a god or goddess appears at the end of a play, it is always to give a divine perspective on the human action (we will see some of the variations of this device in chapter 6). But here it is Medea once again giving *her* version of events. We cannot get outside Medea's manipulative language. She is in control—and coming to Athens, which has offered sanctuary to the murderess. It is essential to the deep moral ambivalence at the end of this play that the heroine is escaping in triumph (and coming to join the community of the audience). The sympathies of the audience have been twisted and turned by the unfolding of the plot—but it is exceptionally difficult not to be both gripped and disgusted by the image of the triumphant mother vaunting the bodies of her murdered children over her husband's despair.

The set of Warner's production was dotted with rubble from building works (as if the palace had newly been completed) and there was a rectangular pool of water center stage. At the end of the play, Warner had Medea and Jason together in the water, locked in an embrace and an exhausted struggle. Her reading of the play had Medea and Jason still erotically or emotionally transfixed by each other, for all their hatred and bitterness (where so many productions see them rather as implacable enemies from the start) (fig. 5). The ending of the play in Warner's production represented the couple still bound to each other in a pattern of self-destructive violence,

5 Fiona Shaw as Medea faces the wrath of her husband, Jason (Jonathan Cake). Where Euripides physically separates the two characters at the climax of the play, in Deborah Warner's production, Jason can just reach out and touch his murderous wife.

unable to separate from each other or to bear each other. This was clearly a deliberate interpretive gesture, but the loss of the vertical axis of Euripides' writing for the stage completely altered the play's final dynamic. It came close to making non-sense of Jason's desperate inability to reach Medea—he could just stretch across the pool. She did not have the children with her, so his pleas for the bodies had no directed focus: why didn't he go into the house and find them? Above all, her triumph became swallowed up in mutual defeat. The fundamental *disjunction* of Medea and Jason, their radically opposite feelings, expressions, and narratives at this point in the play, were lost in a shared embrace. Euripides' construction of a profoundly challenging moral chaos was reduced to an ancient version of *Who's Afraid of Virginia Woolf?*

This production's unwillingness to utilize the vertical axis written into the play left the work finally in the sphere of bourgeois domesticity. A modern audience may find the supernatural conclusion of a dragon-drawn chariot of the Sun too difficult, but what is crucial to the scene is the logic of Medea's self-harming triumph over Jason's impotent despair. The physical staging of Medea soaring above Jason embodies this triumph, and the set that lost all sense of this dynamic destroyed the complexity of the power relations that make the end of the play the challenge it is.

Jonathan Kent's 1992 production of *Medea* starring Diana Rigg (for which she won a Tony in 1994, when the play transferred to New York from London), found a different solution to the problem of the ending, a solution which worked positively with the vertical axis.[6] The set (designed by Peter Davison) was a claustrophobic three-sided courtyard, where the walls were covered with huge metallic panels, one of which made a large central door. The murder of the children was visualized horrifically: one of the higher panels fell from the wall to reveal the children, bloodied and crushed up against a glass inner panel. For Medea's final appearance, all the panels of the upper story of the set fell away with a staggering crash (and a real coup de théâtre). This left Medea revealed, high above Jason, who could not penetrate the lower level of metal panels. On the backdrop behind Medea a film of fast-moving clouds played. As the play finished, she turned her profile to the audience and to Jason. As she stood immobile (like a grand star of the silent cinema), against the rushing sky, the sense of Medea entering a new, more than human existence was powerfully conveyed—without the difficulties of magic dragons, with all their associations of Disney or Wagner. The impotence of Jason and the transformation—the transcendence—of Medea here had a staged, physical expression. Although it is possible to stage the power relations of *Medea* without utilizing the height of the set, the vertical axis gives a particular dramatic form to the hatred and dominance which divide Medea and Jason.

]]] [[[

My final example focuses on the difficulty of the proscenium arch, and shows how the traditional theater can be transformed by a creative design team to produce a modern set which recognizes and works with the central resources of ancient design. The Cambridge Arts Theatre in Cambridge, England, is a conventional English provincial theater, seating 666, with a fixed proscenium arch and standard rows of seating with the barest of raking. In 2004, Annie Castledine directed Sophocles' *Oedipus the King*, with a design by Stephen Brimson-Lewis.[7] The reorganization of theatrical space was an absolutely integral part of what was a hugely successful production.

First, all the external decorations of the proscenium were removed, and the whole was painted the same color as the walls of the theater to blend it as much as possible into the fabric of the building. The stage was turned from a rectangle to a circular form by putting a semicircle of banked seats at the back of the stage (fig. 6). In the middle of this seating, a central door space was created. The front of the stage was extended beyond the proscenium (thrust stage) into the audience to complete the circular acting space. From the front of the stage a walkway was created right across the top of the stalls to the back of the theater (fig. 7). This walkway was used as an entrance and exit, as was the central door.

The effects of this bold design were remarkable. First, the audience, whether seated onstage or in the traditional seats, could constantly see each other. *Oedipus the King* is much concerned with the question of what human identity is, and how we know who we are. It is a play which demands self-reflection at the deepest level—everyone, especially since Freud, is encouraged to see themselves in Oedipus. With this staging, each member of the audience could see the reactions of other

6 The set of *Oedipus the King* at the Cambridge Arts Theatre, 2004. Part of the audience is seated on stage, turning the proscenium theater into theater in the round. The chorus stand on walkways above the audience, as the leader of the chorus enters. The backlighting through schematic columns creates an atmospheric, shadowy central acting space of the city in plague.

7 The set of *Oedipus the King* at the Cambridge Arts Theatre, 2004, viewed from the central entrance during rehearsal. The walkway stretches across the stalls through the circular central acting space.

audience members, and see themselves mirrored. And different parts of the audience had different experiences of the action: their different sight lines revealed different perspectives on the performance. The set encouraged (self-)recognition through looking at others like oneself.

The inside of the house of Oedipus is where the incest and violence have been committed before the play starts and where the violence of the drama itself will take place, namely, Jocasta's suicide and Oedipus's self-blinding. *Oedipus* establishes a strong contrast between Oedipus in his role as king, on the one hand, where he has acted as savior of the state and as a ruler who is widely admired by the people, and, on the other hand, Oedipus as a polluting presence in the state, where his status as family figure—killer of his own father and husband of his own mother—is the source of his own horrific fate and the city's plague. The play opens with him delivering a full-scale political speech to the people, and will end with him as a broken, blinded man being led back into the house. The contrast between the house, again marked by the door through which he enters and leaves, and the public arena, the stage itself, is essential to the play's narrative, and the strong contrast in the Cambridge production between the huge door space and the acting arena made this tension visible.

Oedipus kills his father at the place where three roads meet. He has left what he thinks is his true parental home in Corinth to consult the oracle at Delphi about his parentage. Because he is given an oracle that he would kill his father and marry his mother, he flees away from Corinth, where he has been living—and consequently not only kills his father on the road, but also is led to Thebes, where his mother lives. The play is full of the imagery of roads and traveling. The drama, in showing Oedipus not recognizing the path he is traveling (in all senses), poses a constant question to the audience: do you know what road you are on? Can you tell toward what you are traveling in your life? And it shows again and again that man is mired in ignorance and lack of control. The long pathway across and through the audience symbolized this nexus of ideas. It took the idea of the rampway from the ancient theater and made it a fully integral part of the play's expression of meaning. The long walkway provided a perfect route for the long entrance and exit of Teiresias, the blind prophet whose riddling truths haunt and enrage Oedipus. It also could bring on Creon from Delphi or the herdsman from the outlying land of the king, both of whom also unwillingly bring crucial news that will help in the slow destruction of Oedipus's security. (These three long entrances are so much harder to enact with only a side entrance from the wings of a theater, and none of these characters can sensibly come from within the house.) But it was the way in which this dramatic need for a long, slow entranceway combined with the play's language of roads and traveling that made this staging device so powerfully symbolic.

In any form of theater, a set can release or repress the dramatic power of a script. These masterpieces of Greek drama were written for the particular resources of ancient theater, and the way a modern production responds to these ancient expectations can work to enhance or diminish the dramatic power of the classical tragedies. Each of my four examples shows how. The set of Mnouchkine's *Atrides* exploits the logic of the orchestra in a production where music and collective dancing drive the performance. The *Gospel at Colonus* by contrast resists movement onstage, especially by the chorus, but utilizes the traditional walkway entrances to illuminate a play structured around journeying. The set of Warner's *Medea* understood and recognized the intense focus on the central door (in a way that Mnouchkine's *Atrides* lacked), but in losing the vertical axis of the ancient theater could not articulate the power relations which make the last scene of the tragedy so affecting. By contrast, Kent's *Medea* allowed Medea physically to rise above her humiliated and desperate husband. Castledine's *Oedipus the King* gives a splendid example of how the proscenium arch can be transformed to bring out not just the spatial organization of Greek theater but also the connections between the language of the play and the play's physical enactment—the symbolics of space. To produce a Greek tragedy successfully we have to find the logic of space written into it.

Reading Plays and Seeing Space

So how should these ancient plays be read to reveal their rich sense of place? Each theater, of course, brings its own restrictions and potentialities, just as each designer will have her own imagination and style. Yet each play has its own symbolics of space deeply written into it, and it is a primary task of a director and designer to bring this out.

Take a play like Sophocles' *Electra*, which has been brilliantly produced in recent years in a range of very different productions (including four professional productions in Britain in the 1990s alone).[8] The play begins with three men in the half light of dawn, plotting revenge. Orestes, his friend, Pylades, and the Tutor have returned to Argos to regain control of the house and kingdom usurped by Clytemnestra and Aegisthus. The Tutor has devised a scheme whereby he will spin a false story of Orestes' death so that they can enter the palace and complete the killing of the usurpers. Before putting the plot into action, they agree to go to the tomb of Agamemnon to make offerings to Orestes' dead father to gain his support for their action. As they are about to leave, they hear a woman's scream. Orestes wonders if it is Electra and whether they should stay and see—but the Tutor hustles him offstage. The revenge is all.

This short opening scene establishes a particular and significant frame with typical Sophoclean economy. First, it puts a precise emphasis on the door of the palace, the central entrance. It needs a plot, a dangerous ruse, to gain entry; inside is where the evil queen and her adulterous partner live and where the violent revenge must take place. But, secondly and even more important here, Sophocles is writing *through* Aeschylus. The second play of the *Oresteia*, the *Libation Bearers*, also opens with Orestes and Pylades onstage making a prayer, on this occasion to Hermes to help their enterprise. When they hear Electra and the chorus approaching, carrying the libations for the tomb of Agamemnon which give the play its name, the two men hide to observe Electra's ritual offering. After he has seen his sister's continuing support for her father and his own place in the household, Orestes reveals himself, and the celebrated recognition scene takes place. After this, the two children and the chorus together at the tomb of Agamemnon—centrally placed in the orchestra—sing the great mourning song, to summon support from the dead father. Electra is then sent inside the house while the men commit the revenge. She is to be silent and inside, the correct and proper position for an unmarried daughter in the Greek patriarchal imagination. In Aeschylus's play, the tomb of the father is center stage. It provides the focus for the son and daughter together to appeal for divine support; it acts as a visible reminder of the murder throughout. It brings Orestes and Electra together, to work to save the house. The space of the *Libation Bearers* is articulated precisely between the center of the orchestra, on the one hand, where the tomb of the father is, a religious and ideological node; and, on the other, the door of the palace, marking the inside space and, as we have already seen, the struggle for power between men and women in the house. The ideological work of the play, as it were, is to bring together the tomb and the palace in political and social harmony: Orestes' final terrified exit, pursued by the Furies, indicates in powerfully dramatic terms the failure of that aim.

Sophocles' *Electra* places the tomb offstage. The religious center is removed from visibility. There are two implications of immense importance for understanding the play. First, this is one of several significant silences in this drama. In Aeschylus's play, we are told of Apollo's oracle (and Apollo appears in the *Eumenides* to defend Orestes); the oracle is discussed at length; so too is Orestes' motivation. The great mourning song shows the children together, seeking divine support for their action; there is constant worry about matricide—and it takes a third play and a court case to reach any form of resolution. In Sophocles' *Electra* the oracle is barely mentioned; there is no discussion of the rights and wrongs of matricide; no worries, and no attempt by the children to gain divine support together for the action. This is matricide without commentary. The removal of the tomb to an offstage location is a foundational gesture in this whole-scale shift of moral and political focus. Staging is not merely about what is onstage, but also about what is made absent.

The second implication is equally fundamental. The space for action here has been radically redefined. Where Aeschylus's play established a link between tomb and palace, Sophocles offers the space between them. That is, the center of rule is inside the palace, offstage through the central door; the location of the dead father's lost authority, as symbolized in the tomb, is offstage too. What is left is an in-between space, a space through which to travel, a half place, defined by two absent centers. There is at first sight no obvious reason to be in this space: when Orestes, the Tutor, and Pylades are there it is only because they are on their way to the tomb before visiting the palace. It is an edgy, empty, awkward zone.

It is also Electra's place.

From her first entrance, crying, until nearly the end of the play, when she leaves the stage for merely fourteen lines, she is onstage the whole play. It is one of the longest and most demanding parts in ancient theater (and with precious few modern equivalents for women, too). Throughout the performance she inhabits this strange in-between place in front of the house and away from the tomb. She haunts this area, mourning, weeping, and attacking everyone who tries to cross it. The strangeness of this positioning is repeatedly commented on. "Why are you again out here by the exit of the front door?" demands Chrysothemis—her first line to her sister. Chrysothemis is on the way to deliver offerings at the tomb: she is crossing through. It is Electra who is out of place. So Clytemnestra in her first address accuses her: "Loose again, it seems, you are roaming here." The word "loose" (*aneimenê* in Greek) implies like a wild animal; and as did Chrysothemis, Clytemnestra sees Electra's behavior as a repeated pattern ("again," "again"). A girl should be inside the house, away from public eyes, and certainly not "roaming." Electra is constantly out of place. It is not by chance too that every character in the play tells her to shut up. She is verbally as out of order as she is physically rebelling against the norms of female restraint.

Where Aeschylus's Electra spoke only in prayer and religious ritual—female duties—and was sent back inside as the revenge approached to await marriage in silence, Sophocles' heroine revels in breaking all the bounds of female propriety—and the space she inhabits is the physical embodiment of this.

There is no scene that captures this manipulation of the conventions of theatrical space as well as the moment of the matricide itself. Orestes and Electra have had their brief recognition scene, quickly snuffed out by the Tutor, who is terrified that they are jeopardizing the revenge. The two children together enter the palace. From the *Oresteia* we might expect at this chilling juncture of entrance into the house that the chorus would sing an extended ode on the nature of justice, or on the horrors of female transgression. What we have instead is the shortest ode in all extant tragedy—only fourteen lines—and to our surprise Electra comes back onstage again.

She explains that she has come back out to watch for Aegisthus, but her entrance also creates the fearsome dynamics of the murder scene. For Electra, alone onstage, mediates the action to us in the most unpleasant way imaginable. As her mother cries out in desperation and pain inside, Electra by the door responds, "Someone is crying inside; do you hear, friends?" The chorus break into highly emotional lyric singing in their horror, but as the second cry is heard, Electra, still in the ordinary rhythm and grammar of nonlyric verse, responds, "Look, someone is crying again." The repeated use of the word "someone," as if she does not know who is screaming, is horrific in its dispassionate hate. When her mother begs Orestes for pity, Electra replies, "You showed none for him nor his father," and when Clytemnestra cries out, "Aaargh, I am struck," Electra, with horrifically focused intent on the violent death of her own mother, demands, "Hit her again if you have the strength."

In Aeschylus's *Oresteia*, center stage in the central play, Clytemnestra bares her breast to Orestes and begs, "Respect the breast at which you gave suck, my child"—and Orestes replies with the most famous moment of tragic doubt: "Pylades, what should I do? Should I respect my mother?" and in reply, with his only line of the trilogy, delivered like the word of god, Pylades states, "Count all men your enemies rather than the gods." In Sophocles' play, the mother cries out for pity before the sword of her son, but we do not hear his reply. We do not know if he hesitates. We hear no authorization from Pylades. Instead, we have Electra demanding a further matricidal blow. It is a challenging image of communication in a family destroyed by violence and passion, where Clytemnestra begs her child, who is silent, and the reply comes from Electra, who cannot be heard by her mother: a three-way failed circuit. Instead of moral hesitation and authority, we have silence, and the certainty of hate. The moment of violence in Greek tragedy is often reported via a messenger speech. Electra's commentary is not really a messenger speech or even a description of the events inside. What the audience watches is her contribution to the violence as it happens—her psychological and moral blindness, her ferocity and commitment to revenge.

Electra here again speaks from the strange space that Sophocles has created: neither in the action precisely, which takes place behind the door on the inside; nor from the tomb, where religious support can be sought. This odd place becomes the frame for the twisted and disturbed world of Electra.

The final act of *Electra* is Orestes leading Aegisthus back inside the house to kill him. It is a deeply worrying ending, as we do not know if the Furies will pursue Orestes (as in the *Oresteia* and in traditional versions of the tale), or indeed whether there are any consequences of the matricide. But there is always one last directorial problem: what to do with Electra. Does she go back into the house with Orestes to watch the killing of Aegisthus? This would give her the fulfillment of observing the revenge at first hand, and bring her back into the house, the proper frame for a woman's existence—though it

would be hard not to see her still as an extremely difficult presence in any household. Does she retreat with the chorus, who
have been her support throughout (though often with challenge and distaste rather than simple bolstering)? This would
keep her with the collective of women, offering some image of
potential restoration and integration. But almost all modern
productions have left her alone onstage as the men exit. Hugo
von Hofmannsthal's version, turned into an opera by Richard
Strauss, has her dance herself to death in triumph and annihi-
lation.[9] It is as if Electra has so dominated this space, and been
so associated with it, that it is hard to extract her from it. The
effect on her psyche of her obsession with revenge has been so
intense and so disturbing that without the motivation of hate
and vengeance it is difficult to conceive of her life continuing.
Leaving her onstage leaves her in limbo, a physical incarnation
of the question of how Electra can go on, now.

How, then, has this sense of place been embodied in recent productions? Let me offer two contrasting versions. The
first is another production by Deborah Warner starring Fiona
Shaw in the title role, which opened in London in 1988, and
was revived in 1991. The play was produced in small theaters,
and in the 1991 revival the audience was seated along two adjoining sides of the auditorium. Along the third side was a wall
by which the chorus huddled. The fourth side was the large
door of the palace, in steel. On the stone-floored stage was a
rivulet of water in a channel, and a few stones. Otherwise, it
was stripped down to a bare space. The contrast between the
image of power and technology that the door offered, and the
outside space with the runoff water and stones, was eloquent.
But it was as much Shaw's performance as the simplicity of
the set which defined the space in the terms I have been discussing. Indeed, by 2001, Warner and Shaw saw the production values themselves as dated and overinfluenced by Peter
Brook—but for both of them Shaw's performance remained
the touchstone of the event.

Shaw described what she achieved in this play as a whole new way of acting (I assume she means for herself rather than in the history of world theater). She walked on an edge between madness and sanity, from the first entrance. Her rags were torn and revealed a naked body beneath; her arms were marked with self-harm, and she scratched and pulled at her hair. The performance was, she said, "physically and mentally very dangerous." Her acting ran at a level of intensity and pain that was as far as possible removed from Victorian ideas of "serenity" or "purity" or—a word Shaw despises—"magnificence." Indeed, it was for the audience physically and psychologically difficult to be in the same, small space with Electra. To be so close to such apparent pain and misery and such force of feeling was distinctly uncomfortable (and for some critics altogether too much, though the performance rightly won awards and enormous praise). In this production, at the end Electra was left onstage alone picking up petals or little stones. It was a profoundly ambiguous image: tidying the world for a new order? A pathological emptiness revealed in desperate, repeated gestures? But, above all, it was terribly uncomfortable for the audience, denied any sense of satisfactory closure, any sense that Electra had the release she had promised herself revenge would provide. She was still completely in the space which her lust for revenge and fierce commitment had created for her in the interstices of the power relations of the house.

The simple set proved a perfect canvas for Shaw's performance: Sophocles' portrait of psychological and physical dislocation was starkly, revealingly illuminated. The set was deliberately pared down. It was almost a nonspace in front of the forbidding door, with almost no features. Just a little water to wash off the blood, stone on bare feet . . . This production shows how design and direction, set and acting, are always wholly intermeshed in the finest performances.

My second *Electra* was directed by the young actor and director Jane Montgomery, who had been the understudy for Chrysothemis in the 1991 revival of Warner's *Electra*, and had seen that production many, many times. It is not surprising that her production (at the Cambridge Arts Theatre in England in 2001) showed some influence from Warner's show; my reason for discussing it here, however, is that it was compelled to use a proscenium arch theater, and, partly in response to this, adopted a resolutely modern aesthetic, unlike the realistic style of Warner's company.

Montgomery's production (designed by Michael Spenser) also had a large metal doorway at the center of the back of the set, with a short stairway leading up to it. But in front of this doorway was a huge, underlit petri dish—a circular, flat glass bowl, like those used in chemistry experiments. Electra inhabited this dish. Any character who wished to come in or out of the house had to step into the dish—and thereby spend painful time with Electra. Around the outside of the petri dish were placed four video screens on stands which played memories of Electra's childhood on a repeated loop. The chorus, dressed in wedding dresses, moved in synchronized, mechanized movements, between the screens and on the bare stage: they were not on the same plane as Electra.

Not least because Montgomery's production was in ancient Greek—it was the triennial Cambridge Greek Play, a venerable university institution dating back to 1882[10]—such modernism was a precisely provocative gesture. But what was most striking about the setting was its intelligent attempt to deal with the difficulty of the proscenium arch, and to revitalize Sophocles' particular manipulation of the spatial coordinates of ancient theater. The modernism both broke away from the black box of the proscenium, and found a way of creating a bounded and distinctive arena for Electra's obsessiveness. Neither Warner's nor Montgomery's production made a theatrical arena that looked at all like an ancient Greek theater. But both understood brilliantly how the coordinates written into Sophocles' play for the ancient theater could be instantiated in a modern dramatic space.

Sophocles' *Electra* is a particularly good example for what I have been calling the "symbolics of space." Understanding this play depends first on appreciating its particular use of the physical potential of ancient theater: the door, the stage, the orchestra; and second on comprehending its manipulation of a more ideological sense of space: the threatening associations of women on the outside; the fear of spaces that are neither one thing nor the other; the display of power in the organization of domestic and political spaces. Both of these aspects—the physical and symbolic potential of space—are crucial starting points for any modern production of an ancient Greek tragedy.

]]] [[[

One of the most popular of all Greek tragedies for professional and amateur production since the Second World War is Euripides' *Bacchae*.[11] I don't think it is surprising that the *Bacchae* has proven so attractive, especially from the 1960s onward. Its themes include the tension between wild, irrational emotion and the control necessary for structured social living; the fragile boundaries of masculinity, particularly of the masculine figure interested in his own power and self-control; the power of illusion and transformation to change an image of the world; or, in short, sex, drugs, and power. Yet, although I have seen many productions of this play, and although there have been many influential and often commercially and critically successful versions, I have not yet seen a production which comes close to capturing the full scope of the drama, and to a good degree this is because the play's use of space stretches the resources of the ancient stage to the limit, and all too few modern productions have had the vision to see where the problems of producing a design for this masterpiece lie.

The *Bacchae* utilizes every aspect of the ancient theater. First, the walkways. The play demands that the two old men, Cadmus and Teiresias, leave Thebes at the end of the first scene to go dancing in the mountains, dressed as maenads, that is, as female worshipers of the god Dionysus. Pentheus, the king, himself is led to the mountains, also dressed as a maenad, by the god himself, who is intent on the king's destruction. These two pairs of exits, of men dressed as women, are paralleled in the last part of the play by two returns. Agave, Pentheus's mother, returns from the same mountains, with her band of women, and her son's severed head on her *thyrsus* (the ritual staff carried by maenads). Cadmus himself returns in slow grief with the ripped-apart body of his grandson. Each one of these journeys is hugely different in tone, although each involves people in maenadic costume. Each journey articulates the contrast which the text makes repeatedly between the world of the city and the world of the wild country—between the regulated life in the institutional frames of Thebes, and the untamed, uncultivated, and threatening landscape beyond. "To the mountains, to the mountains!" is the refrain of the chorus, first in ecstatic worship, and then, more frighteningly, as they anticipate and revel in the chase and slaughter of the king. The long exits and entrances are fundamental to how the ritual language of this play spills over into the action. They are like religious processions, first in celebration, but finally in horror. It is not easy to embody these processional paths to and from the wild mountain without a long entrance route in a modern theater. All too often, both the menacing sense of the mountainside—out there—and the ominous religious march to death are lost in the restrictions of a modern auditorium.

The central building is the focus of the middle of the play—and becomes in itself a symbol of the power of Dionysus in the theater. Pentheus has apprehended the stranger

whom he does not know is the god Dionysus and he interviews him onstage. Dionysus is threatening and funny and
seductive and manipulative, and the increasingly irate king
ends up by leading him into the house to be locked into the
stables (which acted as a jail). As the chorus sing, Dionysus's
voice is heard from within (or above) calling his Bacchants,
the chorus of Maenads. As he shouts for the house to be
shaken, and for flames to rise around the house of Pentheus,
the chorus scream that an earthquake is shaking down the
palace, and fire rising from the altar of Semele, Dionysus's
mother. Dionysus emerges unscathed and triumphant from
the jail—followed by a confused and turbulent Pentheus, still
hunting down the escaped stranger, who is standing unper-
turbed on the stage.

In all of Greek tragedy there are few scenes as problematic
as this for a director. We can easily say that this scene expresses
the power of Dionysus and the fragility of man's reliance on
his walls and chains. It displays the failure of Pentheus's control and authority in the face of the god's inscrutable will and
ease of movement. But what is to happen onstage? When the
chorus shout, "Look! Look! How the palace is collapsing!"
what do the spectators see?

There are three main lines that directors and literary
critics have followed. First of all, some have suggested that
there is nothing to see onstage at all, except for the chorus's
emotional reaction to the god's words. Dionysus is the god
of illusion and theater. He can make us see what we need to
see ("Now you see what you ought to see," he says to Pentheus, when Pentheus, possessed by Dionysus, says, "I seem
to see two suns and two cities.") So when the chorus scream,
"Look! Look! How the palace is collapsing!" we are invited
to share the ecstatic vision. The scene is a demonstration of
the power of Dionysus because we the audience, like the characters onstage, are summoned to marvel at theater's power of
illusion, that is, at the power of the god. We celebrate the god

of theater in the theater by surrendering to and wondering at theater's amazing ability to make us believe in fiction, to give ourselves over to illusion. The obvious problem with such a solution is the worry that the audience will just be confused or alienated—and find themselves having a less than celebratory response to the action onstage.

The second route is the path least commonly taken—to take the text at face value and have the palace collapse. So in Roland Joffe's production in London at the Old Vic in 1973 (with a script adapted by Wole Soyinka, the great African dramatist), the set was made up of huge scarlet hanging cloths from the flies. It is a barn of a theater, and the space above the stage is immense. At Dionysus's cry, the cloths were cut and fell, impressively, to the stage, where they lay. The backstage wall and fixtures were visible, and remained so for the rest of the play. There are several problems with such a solution, however. No character mentions the collapse of the palace after this scene, and there is no indication of the sort of reaction, which one might expect to see, to the sudden destruction of the central building of authority in the town. The revelation of the back stage can be distracting (for all its postmodern self-reflexivity), and provides a less than obvious backdrop for the remainder of the play. As with the first solution, the audience's willing suspension of disbelief is set at stake—with equal potential for alienation and confusion.

The third solution is the most mealymouthed. It aims for a small amount of symbolic destruction: the roaring of a flame on an altar, the dislodging of a brick or two, the shifting of a lintel. The disjunction between the chorus's or Dionysus's words, which call out for total destruction and terrifying flames, and such piecemeal and halfhearted chaos is more likely to inspire a smirk from the audience than a feeling of awe. Most generously, we could say that the difference between the words and what is visible again asks the audience to feel the power of divine illusion. But the miraculous, portentous epiphany, described in the language of religious ecstasy, seems likely to be undermined for a modern audience by so feeble an act of destruction.

The house, then, has been cracked and crumbled: but it is into the house that Pentheus and Dionysus go in order to change Pentheus into a maenad's costume, now that he is wholly under the sway of the smiling and dangerous Dionysus. He will come out from within transformed into the image of a female and a celebrant of the god. His self is now as ruined as his house: mined from within by an external force. The earthquake which rocks the palace is a sign also of what will happen psychologically to Pentheus, just as it is of what will happen to him physically, when he is ripped apart by his mother and her sisters. The dissolution of the king—socially, physically, psychologically—is the god's punishment.

So the focus on the house as a symbol of Pentheus's authority and security is very strongly felt. The trick for any director is to find a way of showing the palace to tumble and fall without tumbling and falling. It is a hugely demanding scene.

And it always has been. The first production of the *Bacchae* in Athens was put on after Euripides' death, produced by his son, who found the play in his father's papers. The very first production was faced by exactly the same mystery as every subsequent one. We have no idea what Euripides intended for this scene, and the first performance can be no guide. Like its god, this play is peculiarly hard to shackle.

The orchestra is also critical. This of all Greek dramas is the play least likely to have its chorus cut. The collective band of maenads is so important to the plot that the common device of reducing the chorus to one or perhaps three actors is almost never taken with this play. It would make nonsense of the fear that motivates the action: with the maenads above all it is as a group that the women are terrifying. The chorus sing and dance stunning songs: in quiet celebration of the god, and as bloodthirsty hunters seeking revenge in the name of god. They are described as fearsome and alluring women from the East. And what director would resist the spectacle of a group of possessed Eastern women in animal skins dancing ecstatically? This all requires a place for their performance too, a space for fully Dionysiac expression.

What is more, the final appearance of the god is an epiphany in his full divinity rather than in the disguise of a mortal. That is, he appears at least on the *theologeion*, above the humans, asserting his power spatially as well as in words. When Cadmus complains, "A god ought not be like a human in his anger," he is dismissed by Dionysus with "My father Zeus ordained this long ago." The god is on a different plane than the human beings; and, complain as the humans might, god's authority is inscrutable and all-embracing. Dionysus has been on the same stage as the humans, touching and being touched by them. Finally, he is ascendant.

The *Bacchae* utilizes each and all of the four main resources of the ancient theater. One reason why the play is so hard to produce adequately in a modern theater is the need for long entranceways, a dancing area, a palace which may or may not be destroyed and yet be standing, a raised area for the god's final appearance. It is possible to respect this array of spatial dynamics in a contemporary theater, but all too often one or more aspects are sacrificed and the play falls flat in that area. The *Bacchae* provides the most difficult challenge for a modern director, but perhaps for that very reason it remains one of the most inspiring mountains of theater to climb.

Conclusion

Greek drama is a wordy genre. Whenever any character says, "I have told the whole story," that is always just the beginning of more stories and a lot more laments. There is little action, at least for those brought up on action movies. There are few people who run in Greek tragedy, fewer explosions, and rarely even any physical contact onstage—though when people do touch, it is explosive. This has often led to productions of Greek tragedy that underestimate how deeply physical and spatial the plays are. Any production that has not explored the symbolics of space and movement written into these scripts will end up struggling with the form and significance of the play. These dramas were written for a specific set of resources, which are brilliantly manipulated by the playwrights. The job of a modern director is not to reproduce the conditions of ancient theater but to see how the modern theater can respond to the vividly constructed spatial dynamics of the old plays.

So, first, find your space . . .

Chapter Two
The Chorus

The most distinctive feature of Greek tragedy is also the most vexing for any modern company: the chorus. Every ancient tragedy has its chorus, and every modern production has to face the acute problem of what to do with a group of people onstage throughout even the most intimate exchanges of husband and wife, a group which has long odes in dense lyric poetry to deliver between the scenes of actors acting and events happening. More modern performances fail because of the chorus than for any other reason: if the chorus isn't right, the play cannot work.

The chorus has an image problem. There is nothing more tedious and depressing in theater than a group of actors in white sheets intoning pompous banalities with profound expressions. If a chorus sings and dances, it is hard to shake off the picture of a Hollywood musical (*Seven Brides for Seven Brothers* rather than *Seven against Thebes*). The chorus of the *Oedipus the King* is a chorus of the political elders of the city: how can the Cabinet, as it were, sing and dance without appearing simply ridiculous? Comedy—as Woody Allen's *Mighty Aphrodite* shows—can deal with a chorus more happily, but only through parody and self-mockery. The chorus is an integral part of tragedy, but how can it possibly work in modern theater?

The Ancient Chorus

To answer this question we need first to take a step back and see how the chorus worked in ancient theater—with the aim of discovering how this resource can become an invigorating element of contemporary drama, rather than an embarrassment. As with the question of theatrical space, understanding the principles of the chorus is essential for modern theatrical work.

The basic facts of the ancient tragic chorus are simple and easily expressed. In early tragedy—up to and including the *Oresteia*—a chorus was made up of twelve members. After this, thanks to Sophocles' innovation, we are told, the number was normally fifteen. There was always a leader of the chorus (the choruphaios), who spoke individual lines on behalf of the group. The chorus had a collective identity ("elders of Thebes," "slaves of the house of Agamemnon"), and had matching costumes, including masks (all actors and chorus members were masked in ancient tragedy). The chorus sang and danced odes in between the scenes of the drama. In modern translations it is often hard to appreciate that there are two basic types of verse in tragedy, iambic lines spoken by actors or by the choruphaios, and lyric verse, which was sung. Actors could sing arias, and the choric odes are all sung to the accompaniment of the *aulos*, a double reed instrument. *Aulos* is often translated by "flute," which is quite misleading: the instrument was more like a double oboe and was said to have a great range of sound and to be hugely expressive (unlike the modern flute).[1] In some translations, the choric odes are divided into stanzas called *strophe, antistrophe* and *epode*. This reflects the dancing of the chorus. The standard form of a Greek choral ode is a circular turn to the right (the *strophe*, which means in Greek "turn"); a counterturn to the left (*antistrophe*); and then a standing still (*epode*). The strophe and antistrophe had the same metrical form and matching music and probably matching movements. Each ode was danced as well as sung, in a collective formation. The chorus entered singing to a marching tune, and almost invariably stayed onstage till the end of the drama.[2]

These basic facts are worth knowing, if only to understand what is rarely explained in the translations, but it is far more important to know what the chorus meant within the institution of tragedy and in Greek culture in general. Performance as a *collective group*, first of all, is central to the function of a chorus. One of the structuring principles of tragedy is the tension between the collective chorus and the individual hero. This is visually evident in the contrast between the lone actor on the stage and the group of dancers in the orchestra, but it also goes to the heart of the narratives of tragedy. The hero, especially in Sophocles, is a figure who makes the boundaries of normal life problematic: the hero goes too far, and going too far is *both* transgression *and* transcendence. The greatness of the hero is achieved at the expense of his ability to fit into normal social parameters. The hero is often destroyed—or destroys himself—in the pursuit of his own goals, and this passionate self-belief and self-commitment is set in juxtaposition to the cooperative virtues of the community. The community finds the hero both transfixing and horrific. As with Oedipus in the *Oedipus the King*, the hero is both savior and polluter of the state, a threat and an example, a fearsome enemy and powerful friend. The chorus stands for and dramatizes a communal voice, which is set against the hero's individualism.[3]

We will see something of the variety and complexity in how ancient dramatists utilize this dynamic of individual and collective shortly, but before that we need to look at three important ways that this sense of community is developed: first, through politics and religion; second, through the medium of commentary; and third, through the notion of authority.

There is, first of all, a religious and more broadly social background to the chorus. The chorus was a normal part of the education of young Greeks, an education into the values and stories of the community. Many religious festivals involved a choral performance. A group of young girls or young boys would be selected to train for this performance.[4] A poet was chosen to write a piece for the occasion (or an old and valued work was selected for reperformance), and a choral master taught the group in their collective dancing and singing in preparation for their single performance on the day of the festival. Training was valuable in itself in honing the body and in enforcing collaborative work as a group: the Athenians typically saw this as good preparation for war, and encouraged it as such. But there was a broader cultural import too. Before an audience of citizens, the young, future citizens recited and danced the traditional myths that bound a community together in shared knowledge and belief. The space of the festival is danced into being by the choral movement.

As they grew older, men might take part in other choral competitions. At the Great Dionysia, the festival at which the tragedies were presented, there was also a dithyrambic competition, a contest between the ten tribes of Athens, each of which put in a choir of fifty men to sing a *dithyramb*, a choral song in honor of the god Dionysus. Many states across Greece had equivalent competitions both for boys or girls and for men. So pervasive is the culture of choral singing and dancing that Plato sums up the normal education of the young with a zippy catchphrase, *achoreutos apaideutos*, which means that if you have not performed in the singing and dancing of a chorus, you cannot really regard yourself as an educated or cultivated Greek. Or, "no chorus, no culture."

There is also a specific political frame for tragedy. All our surviving Greek tragedies were produced in the city of Athens in the latter part of the fifth century BCE when Athens was a radical democracy and also a major imperialist force in the Mediterranean. Tragedy repeatedly reveals its genesis within these particular political conditions.[5] It is partly the return of democracy as the banner under which modern states march, together with contemporary anxiety about empire, that has made ancient tragedy so popular a genre again on the Western stage. Ancient tragedy's sense of the paradoxes of democracy and the corruption of imperialism speaks to contemporary politics rather well. Democracy holds up the community as an ideal in a particularly charged way. Democracy demands that the individual act on behalf of the community—especially in ancient Athens, where most political offices were appointed by lot, and where every citizen was required to fight in the military forces of the state, a state which was willingly at war almost every year of the century. "We are of the opinion that the man who wishes to keep himself to himself has no place here," states Pericles, the great general who gave his name to the golden age of Athens, as he celebrates the soldiers who have died for the state.[6] Citizenship comes with duties and obligations: to support the state financially, to contribute to political decision-making, and to bear arms for the state. It is against this background that the institution of the chorus takes on its full weight and significance. The tension between the community and the individual has a special charge in democracy, where the individual is expected to participate fully in the community to the point of giving over his life and livelihood for its benefit. Speaking with a communal voice has a unique force in democracy.

The collective of the chorus, then, brings with it the political, ideological value of the community which democracy brings to the fore, and the religious, cultural value of the chorus in its long performance tradition in Greek society as part of the cultural glue of society. This profoundly affects how the chorus speaks.

The chorus is often seen as providing a sort of commentary on the action—but it is more useful, I think, to say that the chorus always acts as a *hinge* between scenes or between speakers. An ode will always look back to the scene just past, and forward to the action to come. The odes are often difficult, allusive poetry, and the first task of a director is to uncover exactly how the narrative of the ode looks backward and forward. Only in this way can the story of the ode be made clear, its emphases, ironies, and argument. Choral songs, as much as the heroes' speeches, always have an argument. We will need to explore some examples of this shortly, but for the present it is sufficient to make the general case. The chorus offers a commentary on the action that has happened, and looks forward to the action to come, and it does so precisely from the perspective of its collective identity. That is, the chorus mobilizes the *voice of the community*—with the full weight of what community means in democracy and in the shared cultural world of the ancient city.

That is why the choral odes so often turn to myth. The use of myth is not just a literary gloss to the staged action, but a way of setting the action within the frame of traditional stories, within inherited understandings of the world through the narratives of gods and heroes. These other stories provide paradigms of explanation that link the tragic events onstage into the shared world of shared stories. In the same way, the chorus also often expresses a sort of community wisdom. The generalizations which a chorus makes—and which can be so difficult for a modern group of actors to deliver—are a sign of the attempt of the community to make sense of the action through standard moral expectations and social memory. What is less often appreciated is that these generalizations, despite their status as communal and traditional wisdom, are often shown to be quite insufficient to the tragic events unfolding. Not only is life not a bowl of cherries, but, even if it were, it wouldn't explain why a hero is acting the way he is. The chorus struggles, like an audience, to deal with the exceptional disruptions of tragedy, and the day-to-day understanding of the community is one of the first casualties of the world of tragedy. Mundane wisdom is an easy place to retreat to, especially in desperation, but it is scarcely adequate to the horror enacted before the chorus.

The combination of the religious role of the chorus in festivals, the educational role of the chorus in society, and the deployment of traditional myth and moral frameworks within the poetry of the choral odes, together give the chorus of tragedy an inbuilt *authority*. That is, the odes are invested with the status that accrues to social norms. When the chorus speaks we are expected to listen. To hear the voice of tradition. Yet it is also striking that many of the choruses of our extant tragedies are not authority figures—far from it. The majority of plays have as a chorus a group of slaves, or women, or foreigners, or the old (and decrepit)—that is, figures who are marginalized or excluded from the institutions of authority in the ancient Greek world. Of the seventeen surviving Euripidean tragedies, fourteen have female choruses. Indeed, when you have a chorus like that of Aeschylus's *Suppliant Maidens*—fifty half-Greek black virgins who desperately claim descent from Argos, a Greek city—or a chorus like the Eastern Maenads of Euripides' *Bacchae*, it is not easy to reconcile the authority of the chorus with their social marginality, or even social *otherness*.[7]

Yet finding a way to reconcile these two conflicting vectors is precisely what each production of tragedy has to achieve. Each production has to deal with the chorus as a character in itself (as Aristotle puts it in the *Poetics*), and this can vary from a group of raped wives from a destroyed city, to a stressed council of political leaders, to the angry divine monsters, the Furies. At the same time, the production needs to find a place for the communal wisdom which the chorus so often expresses, and the force of religious and moral authority a chorus embodies. Euripides' *Bacchae* is typically extreme: the chorus of Eastern Maenads, who will whoop with triumph when they hear that Pentheus has been pulled apart alive, and who declare "I am no Greek!" sing in one of their earlier odes: "What the common people do, the things that simple people believe, I too believe and do." The combination of radical otherness—murderous, Eastern, female—and the simple religious piety of tradition makes for a particularly heady compound; but this contrast takes to an extreme a tension that exists in all Greek tragedies. Finding the balance between the characterization of the chorus as a particular group, and the traditional, communal authority of the group is one of the hardest tasks for a director to achieve.

The authoritative voice of the chorus has given rise to the two main schools of thought on the chorus through the twentieth century, which have both had a strong influence on modern performance styles. The first, which dates back to the days of nineteenth-century idealism, assumes that the chorus speaks with the voice of the author. It is through the chorus that the author expresses what he actually believes: their authority is from the author. It is, however, always a sign of poor writing or poor directing when we think one character in a play speaks directly for the author, and I have already said enough to show why this view of the chorus is simply untenable. Not only do the chorus regularly misunderstand the action, show themselves to be extreme in their aggression or passivity, and fail to exert adequate influence on events, but all these hesitations and misplaced certainties are also part of the dynamics of the play, not a master voice above it. The "stand and deliver" style of choral chanting often seems to assume that the chorus has some unalloyed authoritative grasp of what is happening onstage. There is no chorus in Greek tragedy that simply sums up or completely comprehends the action: the chorus must remain part of the dialectic of the drama, even when it strives to be more.

The second overarching theory of the chorus is that it acts as an idealized spectator. A chorus, the theory goes, directs the audience's attention, informs us how to react, and acts as an audience on the stage. In a more sophisticated version, the chorus acts more precisely as a dramatized representative of the citizens as a collective. They are us, onstage, so to speak. This helps explain the sense of social memory which the chorus often articulates. But it cannot accommodate the marginal social status of so many choruses, and finds it hard to explain the more bloodthirsty and wild choral odes. It is hard to see fifty half-Greek, black virgins (who go on to murder their husbands on their wedding night) simply as a version of the citizen audience of tragedy (modern or ancient). Directors who reduce the chorus to a single person, or very small group, often have this theory of the chorus in mind. For a modern audience (of bourgeois individuals), after all, a single person can represent the ideal spectator or the citizen view more easily than a group. Constructing the chorus as an ideal spectator or as the perspective of the citizens will inevitably underplay the active role the chorus also plays in the drama as a drama.

So how can we sum up the role of the chorus in ancient theater? The chorus is a collective body, which mobilizes (but does not simply embody) communal wisdom and communal memory. It speaks both as a particular character and with the authority (religious, social, cultural) that comes from its status as a chorus. As a group, it is constantly in significant tension with the individual heroes onstage and their self-commitment. This tension between group and individual is integral to the ideological concerns of tragedy's narratives. The chorus's odes act as a hinge between scenes, and guarantee that tragedy is never merely a sad story but always has commentary, reflection, and distance built into its unfolding.

In short, ancient tragedy is simply inconceivable without the chorus.

The Modern Problem

So why does contemporary theater find the chorus so intractable? Before we turn to the plays themselves and some modern performances to analyze the more successful solutions, we need to specify just what the main difficulties are which face a modern director.

The first problem is the fundamental issue of collectivity. The chorus in ancient Greece emerges from and speaks to a society that is accustomed to collective institutions and, above all, to participating in them, from the Assembly of democracy to the chorus as an educational tool. But what are the modern equivalents? Of course, there are in contemporary society some obvious groups, and some groups which also have an authoritative voice. A council of elders is easily conceptualized through a modern Cabinet or a managing committee from a range of institutions. In religious communities, there are equivalent voices of tradition and elevated status. But it is surprisingly hard to find groups in modern Western culture that are both truly collective and can speak with even a modicum of authority.

The problem is most vivid when productions today aim for modern dress, or a broadly contemporary setting (which is a particularly common response to the more obviously political of Athenian tragedies). In what form can a group of women, for example, emerge as a group, and with a collective voice in such circumstances? The prisoner-of-war plays (*Hecuba, Trojan Women*) can look back to the Second World War to search for a model of a group of dispossessed, traumatized, and terrified women, who find it in themselves to act as a group (with the authority modern society affords victims). But it is much harder to find similar groups even for plays like *Medea*, or *Iphi-*

geneia at Aulis. In Katie Mitchell's 2004 highly moving production of *Iphigeneia at Aulis* at the National Theatre in London, and also in Deborah Warner's production of *Medea*, which I have already mentioned, a group of women with smart, bourgeois dresses and handbags play the female chorus (of local women of Aulis and of Corinth respectively).[8] In Mitchell's *Iphigeneia*, the chorus during the odes danced collectively, a surreal and increasingly hysterical ballroom dance without partners, as they observed the violent preparations for war by the celebrity heroes. In Warner's *Medea*, the chorus was individualized: each woman spoke as herself and for herself, as the odes were spread in prose, without any dancing or change of level of expression, through the chorus. Warner's realism explicitly rejected the chorus's collectivity and the authority that comes with such a communal voice; Mitchell attempted to hold on to a sense of group both in the physical performance and in the recital of the lines. Yet for neither production was there any evident institutional or social frame that quite made sense of the women's presence as a group. Put simply: why were these women there, and in what sense were they a collective, and with what voice could they speak? The realism of Warner and the stylization of Mitchell are both attempts to deal with the chorus, but neither could successfully find a form for the chorus that both had real social roots and which spoke to the dynamic of the play's writing.

A modern production needs to find, then, a role for the chorus that makes sense of the group, and the power with which a group can speak. But it also needs to find an acting style that recognizes the particularity of the chorus's role in the odes. This is the second major problem facing a modern director: the chorus's particular collective voice in action. The odes require the chorus, however engaged in the action, to take a step back into a mode of commentary and reflection: and any performance has to incorporate this shift of expressive level. Choral odes sound different from the debates of the scenes. What is more, the physical role of the chorus in the odes is often undervalued. Their dancing and song has roots in religious processional and sacred performance. Dancing and singing can be a highly risky business in a modern tragic performance: but this does not mean that the play's dynamic of interchange between staged action and choral odes can be simply ignored. The question for modern performance, then, is how to incorporate the principles of the chorus as an institution—without hoping to recapture the lost cultural world of ancient Athenian democracy. How can collectivity and a shift of expressiveness during the odes be incorporated into a contemporary staging?

Modern Solutions: The Full-scale Chorus

Let us look first at three modern productions that have offered productive solutions to these problems through a full-scale chorus, and we can begin with a production I have already mentioned in chapter 1, the *Gospel at Colonus*.

The *Gospel at Colonus* is one of the few productions of Greek tragedy I have seen which had a completely integral and brilliantly effective use of the chorus. The chorus was played primarily by the gospel choir, which was seated in one of the raked banks alongside the entrance stairway (fig. 8). It was, first of all, very much a collective: it sang and responded to the action as a group. But most important, it was a collective that was fully rooted in a social context. Gospel choirs exist throughout the Baptist community; they are brought together and trained as an integral part of a community, and have a history and an existence outside the specifics of this theatrical performance. It is a collective that made instant, recognizable sense as a collective.

The gospel choir traditionally sings hymns, and proclaims the word of God. That is, its songs have an inbuilt cultural authority, and play a part in the maintenance of social

8 The *Gospel of Colonus* in full and exuberant flight. The chorus stand and sing; the singing Oedipuses are ranged around the white piano; the actor Oedipus is seated front of stage; the chorus master is working his chorus into further heights.

memory. The odes of the *Oedipus at Colonus* are particularly suited to this religious framework. The chorus sings praise of Colonus as a holy site; they pray to Zeus for the success of Theseus's expedition to recover Ismene; they reflect on the fragility of mortal life, and the miseries of this world; they hymn the gods of death and the underworld as Oedipus progresses to his fated and mysterious end. The subjects of all of these odes can easily be assimilated to the genre of the gospel singing. The shift toward generalization and moral commentary was easy. The odes made sense as performances by such a choir.

In the Baptist service, the readings of the gospels, prayer, and the preacher's address are interspersed with the singing of the choir, and the choir also responds to the preaching and readings as a congregation (and it directs or encourages the rest of the congregation in such a response). There is an expected change of register from the rest of the service as the choir sings. When the chorus of the *Gospel at Colonus* turned to sing, the shift of expressiveness from the action onstage or from the songs or words of the actors had a coherence that arose from the generic expectation established by the Baptist context.

The chorus of Sophocles' *Oedipus at Colonus* has a remarkably large amount of interactive singing with the main characters, and has an active role at the beginning of the play in particular in trying to stop Oedipus from sitting in the sacred and forbidden area of the Grove of the Furies. The *Gospel of Colonus* solved this by having a group of four male singers (in matching brown suits), who took on the role of the choruphaios and performed the direct exchanges with Oedipus and Antigone. (When they sang "Stop! Go no further!" with synchronized hand movements and in close harmony, they looked exactly like an archetypal early 1970s Tamla Motown group.) The male alto of the group also sang the beautiful solo "Fair-nightingaled Colonus." This bold and complete separation of one man and a small group from the chorus successfully staged Oedipus's interaction with the inhabitants of Colonus as they protected the sanctity of the Grove of the Furies, while also keeping the choir as an undifferentiated group who commented on and observed the story.

The two fundamental problems of the chorus—its collective identity and the expressive voice of the choral odes—were solved here by setting the chorus fully within a tradition of Baptist religious life. This gave a coherent role to the group as a group in the action of the play. And the odes worked as a performance within the frame of a religious service. In almost all cases, bringing Christianity into Greek tragedy brings distortingly anachronistic ideals to bear, but in this case the sheer boldness of the concept and the verve of its enactment transcended the distortion, and it made a great piece of theater.

]]] [[[

Mnouchkine's *Les Atrides* took a completely different route. As with the *Gospel at Colonus*, Mnouchkine's productions have no interest in realism. ("Realism," she sniffs, "psychological drama: that's not art.")[9] *Les Atrides* took its visual and physical inspiration from the theater of the East, specifically the Kathakali tradition of India (with a bit of Bharata and Kûti-yattam added too). Kathakali enacts Hindu myth through song, dance, costume, and narrative.[10] Kathakali literally means "story play," and the importance of storytelling is evident in *Les Atrides*. Kathakali has a lengthy and intense physical training, which is traditionally linked to the preparation of warriors. It produces highly athletic and flexible dancers. The costumes are brightly colored, with elaborate, stylized masks (fig. 9). The Kathakali dance brings together physical movement, music, art, and story in a complete, integrated work which *totalise le sens*:[11] this is a hard phrase to translate because *sens* means both "meaning" and "sense" (as in the five senses). Mnouchkine is trying to capture an experience where ideas and the images onstage come together in a single communication, and affect the audience through their minds and all the senses. In the nineteenth century, under the influence of Wagner, she would have called it a *Gesamtkunstwerk*, a "total work of art."

Kathakali allows Mnouchkine to escape from what she sees as the time-bound, politically unsatisfactory realistic theater of the Western tradition. "The Orient is a memory," she says, "a pathway, a destination. It is in time, in the past, and also in the future, as a concrete ambition. It is also a theater which is very concrete." The Orient is for her a mythical place, a place

9 The chorus of the *Agamemnon* from Mnouchkine's *Les Atrides*, with masks and costumes borrowed from the Kathakali tradition.

of dreams, for all the immediacy and hard work of the theatrical tradition; it produces a theater, which, unlike the *Gospel at Colonus*, is precisely *not* rooted in the traditions or the here and now of the audience, nor is it even a familiar form to her expected audience. Yet it does enable her to produce a coherent and integral world where "story play" and physical theater come together.[12]

So, Mnouchkine's chorus for the *Agamemnon* enters with a springing dance, but then sits in a geometrical pattern, each in a billowing skirt, to tell the first long story of the trilogy, the opening choral ode. The odes become a form of storytelling, one of several types of narration (as well as action) in the trilogy. They are marked out as a particular genre of speech-act, which is coupled closely with the collective dances they perform. They are a group by virtue of their collective dancing and storytelling: they do not need a precise set of cultural markers as a group because the whole mise-en-scène of the drama is removed from modern culture into the special, fictional world of Kathakali story play. Mnouchkine's chorus, then, responds powerfully both to the collective force of the ancient chorus, and to its special mode of expressiveness, but does so precisely by rejecting the lure of audience familiarity or institutional recognizability.

]]] [[[

Mnouchkine is careful not to call her chorus "timeless," for all that she creates a chorus removed from the world of her audience. There is a long history of regarding Greek drama as timeless, which was especially influential in German Romantic thinking. The appeal to a timeless world is a further way in which directors have attempted to deal with the problem of the collectivity of the chorus: separated from a specific historical frame, there is, it is thought, no need to create an institutional idea of the chorus as a group. It is actually rather hard to keep a fictional world "timeless," as the present slips into any fiction all too easily and all too often without recognition. Ancient Greek warriors in eighteenth-century costume populate the art of the eighteenth century, just as the "timeless" world of the fairy-tale seems to be permanently inhabited by the nineteenth-century German culture of the Brothers Grimm. ("Timeless" always really means "timeless, for the here and now.") What is more, the third play of the *Oresteia*, the *Eumenides*, brings the mythic action into the contemporary world of fifth-century Athens, with references to the procedures of the law court, to recent military treaties, and to current political turmoil. It is a play in which every generation has seen a reflection of its own politics of gender and of social justice.[13] So in *Les Atrides* the integral world of Kathakali was punctured in the final play by a strong sense of contemporary politics, as the choruphaioi appeared as bag ladies (which is not a Kathakali type). This link to the contemporary is certainly not alien to the *Oresteia*. But the conjunction of the Kathakali mythic narrative with Mnouch-kine's modern, self-aware, ideological positioning made for a difficult transition.

A second version of the *Oresteia*, the famous production by Peter Hall with Tony Harrison's translation in 1981 at the National Theatre in London, used the ancient technical device of the mask to help create an idea of the timeless in a particularly impressive way.[14] This staging had a full-size all-male chorus, and they wore stylized, austere masks, designed by Jocelyn Herbert. The production aimed at a form of timelessness in that the costumes and set had no particular cultural location. For this, the masks were crucial.[15] They were identical, and had the effect of depersonalizing each actor (which some of the actors found disconcerting—as did some of the audience, who could not tell which chorus member was speaking any particular line). It took a good number of weeks in rehearsal to become accustomed to the brute object itself, and it was striking that the actor Greg Hicks, who played Orestes, managed to develop a stunning expressiveness by the use of gesture and the angling of the mask into and out of the light that few other members of the cast achieved. Masks, like dance, can be used to help establish the collectivity of the group, but they are fiendishly difficult for a modern cast to work with.

Peter Hall is one director who is fascinated by the potential of masks. He has called them (rather bafflingly) the equivalent of the Shakespearean iambic pentameter—by which I take him to mean that masks are both the very life-breath of Greek theater and a necessary discipline that serious actors need to train hard to master, and it is only with such slowly achieved mastery that they can become the flexible, expressive tool that they are capable of being.[16] The mask can be potent in unexpected ways. *Tantalus*, written by John Barton and directed by Peter Hall (in what was a very stormy process from script to stage), is not a Greek tragedy—it has, in fact, very little of the conflict that makes tragedy so affecting; it is, rather, a loose-knit modern retelling of some Greek myths over ten plays and a whole day and night in the theater.[17] But the cast and chorus for the first performance in Denver, Colorado, and later in England were masked. In one of the most affecting scenes, the chorus of Trojan women prisoners of war were stripped naked and branded. It would be brutal enough to have such a scene staged under any circumstances (and the chorus afterward talked of how they had felt humiliated by their loss of voice in this scene in particular),[18] but the fact that each face remained masked while the body was wholly naked added to the unpleasantness of the scene considerably. The combination of the stripped and all too individual bodies, with the abstract distancing of the masks, each the same, raised nasty questions for the audience (and the cast) about sadism, voyeurism, and the depersonalization of torture. Masks change the relation of the actor to her own body, as well as to any psychological, individual motivation, and they also change the relation of the audience to the cast members. They can be deeply effective, especially in creating the collectivity of a chorus, but they also require a training and sensitivity that few companies allow and few actors have been prepared for.

Modern Solutions: The Reduced Chorus

In the three productions I have just discussed, the *Gospel at Colonus*, *Les Atrides*, and the Hall/Harrison *Oresteia*, a full-size chorus, with a developed sense of collective identity, was an integral part of a rigorously nonrealistic theatrical aesthetic. Yet many modern productions take their starting point from the extreme passions of Greek tragedy and seek to follow the bitter familial and political arguments as human stories within a Western realistic tradition.

Fiona Shaw's performance of Electra is a good case in point. The play focuses on the psychological torment (and the political implications of such torment) of a single lead character, who dominates the play and its emotional world. In this production the chorus was reduced to five women, who regularly huddled to one side of the stage. (Richard Strauss, in his opera *Elektra*, has three maidservants sing a few taunting lines at Electra in the opening minute of the opera, but otherwise dispenses with any chorus at all, a pointed gesture in a genre which regularly employs a chorus—and one which set the tone for twentieth-century *Electra*s.) In Warner's scenario, the chorus becomes some older friends of Electra. They cajole and advise her, and back off from her extreme emotion. The choral odes, split between the different members of the chorus, become a conversation which rehearses their shared notions of right and wrong, the stories of the past, and their hopes for the future—as friends might be prompted to do.

David Leveaux's production of *Electra*, starring Zoë Wanamaker (London and New York, 1997–98—another emphatic critical success) took this a step further.[19] He had a single actress deliver all the chorus's lines (which were significantly cut in the translation he used), along with two silent women, who acted as a sort of physical shadow to Electra and the chorus leader. What cannot be captured by such a scenario is the full sense of the collective against which the individual Electra is to stand out, nor can we expect such a chorus to dance religious space into existence. Such a chorus cannot easily represent the religious or social community. But within such limitations, the chorus's role did not jar with the emotional rawness of Wanamaker's performance, and, indeed, it provided a necessary backdrop to the otherwise unmitigated familial horrors of the play.

But reducing the chorus brings its own problems. Jonathan Kent's production of *Hecuba* at the Donmar Theatre in London in 2004 was a huge critical triumph, due in large measure to Clare Higgins's exceptional emotionally draining performance as Hecuba.[20] The Donmar is a very small theater (which has produced some of the most important performances and performers of the last thirty years), with seating on three sides of a tiny stage. There is no room onstage for a chorus of fifteen, even if Kent had wanted such a team. The aesthetic of the production was largely realistic: the stage was a rough seashore, with the mouth of a tent to the rear, and with a long and broad pool of water along the front of the acting area (designed by Paul Brown). It opened with a real coup de théâtre as the ghost of Hecuba's son, Polydorus, emerged with wonderful illusionist magic from within the middle of the pool. The chorus was perhaps the least satisfactory part of the production, however. The choruphaios was played by a single woman, who delivered the link lines between speeches and who helped lift Hecuba when she fell. She was basically a character in the play, another Trojan prisoner of war. Consequently, she had an individual's foibles, peculiarities, and engagement in the action. She could not speak with choral authority, or offer the contrast a choral group offers to the lead actor. High on the back wall there was a platform, where, from the moment the audience came in, another woman stood, writing names on the wall, adding to a list, which covered the whole backdrop. These were names of the dead in war, and included modern names from contemporary war zones. Occasionally, this woman would sing, in mournful and inarticulate manner. The choral odes were largely cut. The chanteuse, without words, could only produce a musical backing track to the action—emotionally riveting on occasion, but never a commentary or articulate response. The focus on the principle actors was intensified by this directorial decision, but a dynamic of Euripides' writing was also lost. In particular, the chorus sings of a longing for other places and other times, and a memory of their collective lost past. This emotional window out of the grimness of the camp could find no voice.

In their first ode, for example, Euripides' chorus sings plaintively of the wind that will blow their ships to a new home, as they imagine the holy places of Greece. Their evocation, with a twinge of hope, summons up a landscape which contrasts with the ruins about them, although their song finally collapses into misery at their fate as slaves. Their collective evocation contrasts with the singularity of the queen, who will not find a new home in Greece, who will not passively be taken to a new home, who cannot find any hope.[21] Hecuba's extreme and particular response to her situation is fully articulated against the group, and their singing about other places, peaceful places, takes the play temporarily away from the brutality all around. All of this is lost when the lines are cut and the chorus becomes a single confidante.

The splitting of the roles of the chorus in this case (unlike in *Gospel at Colonus*) did not allow any sense of a collective presence, or a communal memory, to develop, nor a shared moral ethos to find expression. The chorus's role was essentially neutered, reduced to a bare functionalism in the case of the choruphaios, and a token, symbolic gesture for the chanteuse on the platform. Here, the chorus has lost the lifeblood that makes sense of its presence in the play.

]]] [[[

Finding the role and the identity of the chorus is a fundamental challenge for any modern production of ancient Greek tragedy. The full-scale chorus needs to develop a coherent collective presence which makes sense within the aesthetics and narrative of the drama. Even the reduced chorus needs to seek a role which allows it to speak with the authority of a chorus, and which allows it to step into the special style of narration of the choral odes. Solving this basic problem is one of the director's most important tasks. When choral odes are savagely cut from the script, when the chorus becomes a single actor, when a group onstage simply stands and emotes at the audience, the dynamics of the chorus have been lost, and the production will almost certainly find itself wallowing. It is unfortunately a rather common theatrical experience.

Music and Dance?

Music and dance defined choral performance in the ancient world. It is part of the way that the choral odes are marked out from the scenic action. There is a very long history in the West of exploring how music and dance can form part of a tragic aesthetic. The beginnings of opera in the Renaissance were explicitly an attempt to reinvent the experience of Greek tragedy, and Wagner in the nineteenth century created the Bayreuth Festival as his version of an ancient Greek festival and the *Ring* cycle as his tragic work of art. Mendelssohn's music for *Antigone* was some of the best-known music in the nineteenth-century repertoire (though scarcely heard today). How, though, has modern theater responded? How should a modern performance deal with the different form of expressiveness offered by a choral ode?

I have already mentioned the music of *Gospel at Colonus* and *Les Atrides* as the driving force behind each of those productions. As we have seen, both directors, Ariane Mnouchkine and Lee Breuer, worked closely with the musical team to create a performance where the music was integral to the drama as narrative and as aesthetic experience. In both cases, the music was located within the cultural context of the drama: the gospel music for the Baptist service, the Asian-style percussion music for the Kathakali. We have also discussed successful productions which have no music or dance, and for which music and dance would seem wholly alien: the Warner/Shaw *Electra*, for example. Defining the role of the chorus goes hand in hand with finding the chorus's voice and physical style in the odes.

It is easy to recognize the mistakes, after the event at least. Vanessa Redgrave's performance as Hecuba in London, Washington, and New York in 2005 received very mixed reviews, and had a stormy progress.[22] The production sacked the director, Laurence Boswell, between London and Washington, and asked the poet Tony Harrison, who had translated the play, to rework the production for the United States (and certainly the cast was not happy with the show midrun in London when I saw it). One of the most striking aspects of the London production was the music composed by Mick Sands. The chorus sang the odes (and sang well), but the style of the music is perhaps best described as modern "serious musical": *Les misérables* for a chorus of traumatized prisoners of war. It was extremely difficult for the cast to escape from the negative associations of transatlantic triviality and a happy ending that the style of music evoked. The music deflated the tragic narrative.

By contrast, Katie Mitchell's production of the *Phoenissae* for the Royal Shakespeare Company in 1995—the first time this play was produced on the professional stage in Britain—turned to the Balkans for its music.[23] This has proven a trend-setting decision, and a whole host of productions have since taken the same route. This style of music has several advantages. First, it is sung by groups of women in circumstances other than in the theater. One difficulty with the music for the Redgrave/Harrison *Hecuba* was that its style is a musical form which is seen *only* in the theater, and immediately recalls only theatrical experience, and thus distances the audience from an emotional engagement with the staged action. Second, the Balkan music is traditionally sung by women not just at social gatherings as a form of narrative or relaxation, but also at intense social moments of despair or joy: at funerals, weddings, scenes of protest and celebration. This means that the music can easily be adapted to the range of emotions which a chorus can express, from prayer, to triumph, to despair, to storytelling, to calls for revenge. Third, the music arrives for a modern Western audience with associations of a distanced, passionate, traditional society. This is, of course, no more than a stereotype, but it is an image that positively aids response to the tragedy. From images of funerals especially, it is a music associated with intense and sincere grief. Fourth, because it is a so-called folk tradition, it comes invested with a sense of a history stretching back into a mythic time. It does not have a specific or precise historical setting to jar with the staged narrative.

Mendelssohn's music for *Antigone* would sound extraordinary now to a modern theater audience. No doubt, Balkan music will be seen to be a particular fashion with the benefit of hindsight. But the general lesson which the success of Mitchell's *Phoenissae* reveals is important. Music for tragedy needs some rooting in a social form outside the theater; it should respond to the wide range of expressiveness a chorus displays; it has to be adapted to the role of the chorus: a collective chorus needs music that comes from a sense of that collective.

In ancient Greek theater itself, the chorus came to have less and less to say. The later scripts of Euripides in general have a much more restricted role for choral song than we find in Aeschylean drama. By the time of the fourth-century, the chorus was no longer an integral part of the play, and repertory companies traveled without a chorus. The stars acted, and in between the scenes a local chorus would sing what it had been trained to sing. But for all our surviving tragedies the chorus is integral and the odes essential to the play's meaning and to the unfurling of its narrative. If the chorus is not thought through, the play will stumble.

Finding the Role of the Chorus

Finding the role—the identity and voice—of the chorus is, then, the biggest challenge and the biggest stumbling block for the modern director. So how can this role be discovered?

Talking, as we have, of "*the* chorus" of Greek tragedy has been useful for bringing to light the general problems which face any modern production. But one danger of such a discussion is that it conceals just how varied the treatment of the chorus is from drama to drama, and how carefully each play needs to be read to find the identity and voice of the chorus. To finish this chapter, I want to look at just three examples, which will help demonstrate this variety and the range of dramatic potential in ancient tragedy—and also give an indication of how the chorus's role *can* be productively thought through.

My first example is Euripides' *Trojan Women*, a play which has been produced many times in the twentieth century in response to the wars and suffering which have so ravaged modernity. Gilbert Murray's translation toured Europe after the Great War (it had already had an effect during the Boer War),[24] and Euripides' focus on female suffering as the consequence of male fighting has made it a favorite of recent decades too.

The plot is simple: the Trojan women are in a transit camp (the space of this play is precisely a nonlocation, an arena marked by lost coordinates). The city has been captured and is about to be burnt; the women are about to be sent as slaves to Greece. Hecuba, former queen of Troy, is visited by three former princesses: her daughters Cassandra and Andromache, and Helen, the cause of the war which has destroyed Troy. Cassandra, a divinely possessed prophetess, who always tells the truth and is never believed, is being sent as a spear-bride to Agamemnon: she enters singing a triumphant wedding song, and argues with sophistic brilliance that losing the war was better for the Trojans than winning it was for the Greeks. Andromache, wife of the dead Hector, is to marry his murderer's son. In the course of her scene, when she thinks she has reached the nadir of misery, she is forced to realize that she has not yet begun to grieve, as the Greeks come and take her child away to be killed. Finally, Helen argues with Hecuba before Menelaus, Helen's first husband, that she cannot be blamed for the Trojan War or for her adultery. Each scene is about the reversals of fortune, about a woman's role in relation to men and marriage, and about where true grief and true cause for blame lie. This is all set under the shadow of a divine prologue, where Athene, the former great supporter of the Greeks, announces that she will destroy their fleet on the way home. The victors in their turn will be victims.[25]

It is a play which mixes utter grimness with moments of unbearable laughter, intellectual arguments with painful emotion. It is extremely hard to control the tonal variation. Although Hecuba is present throughout, visited in each scene, there is no doubt that the chorus has to bear a considerable weight in the unfolding of the drama, and it is the chorus which gives a tonal grounding throughout, the baseline, as it were, against which the scenes resound.

Their basic role is clear enough: a collective of women, raped, terrified, and desperate after having lost their homes and families forever. Hecuba is onstage from the start; she sings a lone song of despair and the chorus enters from different sides in small groups to join in an antiphonal song of mourning. The separate entrances and separate voices gradually becoming a chorus *performs* the construction of the group a group: we see how the women come together in mutual recognition and consolation. The fragility of this chorus is essential to their emotional singing, and this opening sets the tone for their performance throughout.

Their first ode, sung in response to Cassandra's bizarre prophecies, begins with a surprising invocation of the Muse. There is no other tragic ode where this happens, though it is a commonplace of epic poetry. It is as if they are trying to comfort themselves by seeing themselves as the suffering victims of epic, as if by telling their story as an epic poem they can salvage something from the wreckage of their lives. The ode tells of the arrival of the Trojan horse and vividly depicts the scene: "The people stood high on the rocks of Troy and shouted, 'Go, our troubles are over, go bring this holy image into Troy to our goddess.' What young girl, what old man did not run from their houses . . ." But the misplaced happiness turns rapidly to destruction, and the narrative switches to the first person, as the women recall how "beloved children snatched at their mothers' dresses with fluttering hands. War was stalking from his hiding place." The song hits home, as the recognition of the ruin of their own lives, their own homes, destroys any epic distance from the story of loss. It is precisely at this point that Andromache enters, clutching her child, soon to be destroyed, the visible sign of the violence of the Greeks and the misery of the women.

The ode maps two trajectories, then. It begins from Cassandra's last long prophecy and wild joy with a note of epic poetic control, but it moves into a more personal lyric that introduces the next scene of mother and daughter keening together. It begins with an apparent attempt to console each other, and ends with a description of horror and loss. Both in the shape of its narrative and in its emotional content the ode moves away from control toward misery, a failure of shared consolation. In both these ways, this song is a perfect example of what I have called the choral ode as "hinge."

The second ode is sung after the Andromache scene and its terrible collapse into despair with the impending slaughter of her small son, Astyanax. It tells in the first two stanzas of how Hercules had been the first to sack Troy, when he had been cheated of his reward for rescuing the king's daughter. The chorus in their misery revert to myth, to their shared cultural memory, "the old stories." The tale combines another narrative of destruction of their city by Greeks, with a lingering hope that, as then, so perhaps now the city might rise again. It takes the chorus away from current misery into the world of the past, though even there destruction lurks. This is the double work of consolation: another story of pain, designed to lessen current woe. It performs the desperate sharing of grief over time. The second two stanzas, however, tell of another ravaging of Troy, when Ganymede, a beautiful Trojan prince, was snatched by Zeus to be his cupbearer on Mount Olympus. This leads them to reflect on the power of sexual desire, and how Zeus's love for a Trojan prince linked them to the gods, the very gods who have now deserted them. "God's love for Troy is gone," are their final words. The mythic tale comes up hard against the present with another eruption of loss and despair. What is more, their song of sexual desire and ravaging introduces the arrival of Menelaus, and the erotically charged appearance of Helen. Again, this time through myth, the ode has an internal narrative from past to present which traces an inescapable pattern of destruction; it also acts as a hinge, looking back to the Andromache scene's powerful depiction of despair and loss, and forward to the sexy Helen. Again, the chorus's shared consolation is fragile and leads directly to a further twist of their pain.

The final ode, after the newly besotted Menelaus has led off the hated Helen to his ship, begins significantly with betrayal. How could Zeus have betrayed the temples of Troy to the Greeks? This starts a long lamentation, a mourning first for the sacrifices and choruses of the religious festivals, then for their husbands, and finally an outpouring of fear for their life as slaves in Greece. After the witty and virulent argument between Helen and Hecuba, it brings the play back to the rock bottom of the women's misery (as it also introduces the arrival of the little body of Astyanax for burial). It acts as a headpiece to the final act of the play, the slow, mourning departure of the women from their destroyed city.

Each of these three central odes has its own narrative pattern, and each acts as a hinge between scenes. Together, they provide a portrayal of a group of women coming together to form a fragile group, attempting to console each other, by shared stories and shared mourning, collapsing back into grief and anger and the silence of trauma. The chorus construct a constantly flowing picture, which runs through the whole play and against which the individual characters act out their strategies of survival, gestures of condolence, and collapse into despairing silence. Together, the chorus and the main characters express a harrowing image of the aftermath of war that has made this play one of the most frequently produced of Greek tragedies in the modern era.

My second example can be treated more briefly: Aeschylus's *Eumenides*, the third play of the *Oresteia* trilogy. The chorus of the *Agamemnon*, the first play of the trilogy, is a group of old men, who bring the authority of age to their storytelling and the incapacity of age to their response to the murder of the king: when the king's death cry is heard they split into twelve separate voices, none of which can decide what to do. The splitting of the chorus mirrors the social disorder of the regicide, the disruption of community. The chorus of the *Libation Bearers* is a group of female slaves, who accompany Electra on her mission to the tomb of Agamemnon. They have a direct effect on the action, however, because when the Nurse comes out to summon Aegisthus back to the palace, the chorus persuade her to change her message, so that Aegisthus walks into the trap without the bodyguard with which he had made his first entrance at the end of the *Agamemnon*. In the *Eumenides*, the chorus becomes a full player in the action.[26]

The Furies, who make up the chorus of the *Eumenides*, are wakened in the Temple of Apollo by the ghost of Clytemnestra. They are chased away by the god, Apollo. They pursue Orestes to Athens. They sing there a binding song—a magic incantation—to keep him bound to the altar of Athene. They appear as the prosecutors in the law court. Finally, they negotiate a new home for themselves in Athens with additional duties, and join the great final procession to the Acropolis.

Unlike the chorus of the *Trojan Women*, who are captured and passive victims, the Furies run, jump, shout, argue, and march. Above all, they engage all the actors in direct confrontation, debate, and physical interaction. This is the very epitome of what Aristotle meant when he said the chorus should be a character in the drama.

Their entrance song is a song of anger at what they perceive as their outrageous mistreatment; their final song is a celebration of the potential of the city of Athens. In between, they sing two long odes. The first is the "binding song." This song is actually the performance of a ritual, an incantation, which binds Orestes under their power. Here, we have song *as* action: the power of words on display. Choruses do indeed perform prayers, formal laments, conjurations. The chorus, as I have already mentioned, has in itself a religious aspect, and with such songs that are in themselves ritual, the chorus enacts a role that a chorus could have outside the theater.

The second long ode of the Furies is a reflective consideration of social justice and the role of divine authority in the human world. It is extremely general and acts as a prelude to the law-court scene to follow. "Praise neither anarchy nor a life under tyranny. God grants power to the middle course in everything," they sing with exemplary common sense. The wild and threatening monsters of the opening of the play sing now as contemplative political thinkers. I do not think that it makes sense here to see this in a modern way as a "change of character." Rather, this is an excellent example of the tension between the two roles of the chorus—as particular group and as generalizing, authoritative institution of the city. When the chorus of Furies are finally incorporated into the city as guardians of ethical order, the two roles of the chorus will come together. What we see here is a crucial juncture in the development of this figuration. As audience, we are observing through the role of the chorus the assimilation of the violent desire for revenge into the institutional order of the city. The common tension between the two roles of the chorus is here made part of the play's very thematic structure. The *Eumenides* is unique in giving the chorus such an active, varied, and significantly developing role within the drama.

There are formal similarities between the chorus of the *Trojan Women* and the chorus of the *Eumenides*. But the differences are far more striking. The subtle flow of the Trojan women's traumatized attempt to find a collective voice and some comfort in their despair contrasts powerfully with the monstrous, wild, but political Furies, a violent, articulate, divine force in the city. The contrast reveals just how much scope there is in the dramatic power of the chorus for a director's skill and vision. But it also reminds us how easily an unimaginative or uncomprehending treatment of the chorus will crush a performance.

My final example is from a play less often produced in modern times, though its interest in self-deception, in a fantasy of revenge, and in the power of myth, which together cause awful violence, should make it a promising candidate for revival: namely, Euripides' *Electra*. In this version of the Electra story, Electra has been married off to a farmer on an outlying farm (again the space of the play is very precisely defined, and as with Sophocles' *Electra*, the contrast with Aeschylus's *Libation Bearers* is pointed and significant). The farmer, however, has not slept with the princess out of respect for the proper order of things. Electra's first entrance is with a water jar, going to the river to fetch water, a menial task her husband tells her that she need not undertake. The entrance with a jar is an obvious visual joke on the *Libation Bearers*. This Electra is just getting water for the household, not engaged in a ritual act of purification of the dead. What is more, the fact that she insists on getting water and complaining about it, when there is no need, indicates her capacity for self-dramatization that will become all too evident as the plot unfolds. The chorus's entrance follows on this. It is an excited group of young women who have come to announce the festival of Hera and to encourage Electra to come with them.

The basic identity of the chorus, then, is not hard to outline. They are the town's girls on their way to a religious festival—a chorus, as it were. Once again, the dramatic chorus's general religious function overlaps with their particular dramatized religious role in the play. Yet here they enter also in order to make an eloquent contrast with Electra. They are keen to celebrate the goddess and to take part in the community's worship; she has marginalized herself, and refuses to participate. Where they respond simply to her self-pity by offering her fine clothes and jewelry to attend the festival, she demands to wear rags and to shave her head in mourning—and yet will complain to the disguised Orestes that she is forced into this drudgery and humiliation. Electra's self-dramatization as victim is sharply highlighted by the happy and straightforward girls on the way to the festivities.[27]

This sense of contrast comes to the fore in their first ode, the only song I will discuss here. After the disguised Orestes has been welcomed into the farmer's hut for humble but honest hospitality—much to Electra's annoyance—the chorus, alone onstage, sing an ode on the background of the Trojan war, and in particular an evocative description of the decorations on the great shield of Achilles. This does lead toward a brief final hope for the punishment of Clytemnestra, but the ode has often been criticized for its tenuous relevance to the plot. In narrow terms, the connection *is* tenuous. What the ode invokes, however, is a glamorous epic past of military virtue and heroic valor, which stands in poignant juxtaposition to the poor hut of the farmer and the squalid emotions of Electra.

This juxtaposition of epic glory and the squalor of the present fits well into the play's concerns. *Electra* is much taken up with how stories passed down from the past—myths—lead men to commit crimes by offering false models. The desire to be a hero can blot out moral sensitivity or basic decency. Electra's self-dramatization is part of this critique of self-deception. The first choral ode harks back to an ideal and idealized past, and this image of heroism echoes through the play. What may seem at first like an ironic counterpoint to the farmer's life becomes a much darker worry as the children persuade each other to take up the mantle of heroism and murder their mother.

This is a perfect example of what I have called the different voice of the chorus. Here is a chorus of young girls who have been chatting about the festival they are visiting and who have been trying to persuade Electra to dress up and join them for the celebration. Now, alone onstage, this group sings an ode about the epic past and a hero's shield. What they sing has the authority of tradition—putting into circulation a shared and known story, to be listened to and reflected on. The ode makes sense primarily because it contributes to the themes of the play in an abstract way. It is hard to see it as a naturalistic moment, as the sort of song a group of girls might sing on their way to a festival. It is almost as if they step out of character, and find another voice.

A modern production needs to find a style for the chorus that can capture both this generalizing, abstract voice, and the voice of a vividly characterized group of girls. Consistency and continuity of character is a standard aim of contemporary acting. The chorus's ability to shift between a more naturalistic engagement with the action, and a more abstract reflection of it is a particular challenge, both for the director and for the audience. This "shifting voice" is an essential dynamic of the chorus.

These three plays are great examples of the immense variety we can see in the three crucial aspects of the chorus's role: the relation between the collectivity of the chorus and the individual commitments of the actors; the narrative flow of each ode, including the relation between the ode and the surrounding action; and the shifting of the voice of the chorus. Between the raped slaves of the *Trojan Women*, the terrifying Furies, and the carefree girls of the *Electra*, the range of characterization in the role of the chorus of tragedy demonstrates the dazzling technique on show in the tragedians' writing for the chorus. Learning to appreciate this technique is part of the necessary experience of a director of Greek tragedy.

Conclusion

It would be possible to go through every tragedy in this way to write its choral score, as it were—tracing its sense of identity, its interaction with the actors, the narrative of the odes, the relation of the odes to the action. It would also be possible to do so in greater detail and more depth than I have attempted here. But that would be the work of directing a chorus. What I have tried to do here is to lay out some of the problems which the chorus poses to the modern director, and to explore the parameters of how these problems can be overcome. What cannot be stressed strongly enough, however, is that the chorus can be an extraordinary and thrilling theatrical resource. With an understanding of the principles underlying the chorus and with an appreciation of the subtlety and variety of the writing for the chorus, a director of real imagination is offered an opportunity and a challenge to bring to life the very heart of Greek tragedy.

Chapter Three
The Actor's Role

For an actor trained in modern theatrical techniques, or for an amateur actor approaching ancient theater perhaps for the first time, Greek tragedy can be a disconcerting experience. The texts often can seem starkly formal, with long, rhetorical speeches interspersed with neat one-line exchanges. Many speeches, where one might expect an intimate or personal discussion, seem to veer into political or philosophical reflections. Searching for motivation or character development through modern psychological expectations can prove a frustrating effort. The result has often been dire: actors standing still and barking pompously at each other, aiming at some sort of "grandeur"—these are the classics, after all—or emoting embarrassingly unengaging expressions of grief.

This chapter will look at some of the basic problems of acting Greek tragedy, through the three basic categories of physical action, speaking of words, and development of character. This is not an acting manual, but understanding these basic issues may help a company find some routes through to a more satisfying experience in rehearsal and onstage.

No Tea, No Telephones: Physical Action on the Tragic Stage

Let me begin with an insight that Clare Higgins offered after playing Hecuba to great acclaim in London in 2004. The first and founding problem, she said, for an actor facing Greek tragedy is that there are no chairs and no telephones.[1]

This brilliantly sums up one of the basic differences between modern and ancient theatrical writing. Take a play like *The Importance of Being Earnest* (which for a classicist like me may pass for the modern). The scene is "Morning room in Algernon's flat on Half-Moon Street. The room is luxuriously and artistically furnished. The sound of a piano is heard in the adjoining room." The play begins with "Lane . . . arranging afternoon tea on the table, and, after the music has ceased, Algernon enters." The dialogue opens with Algernon talking languorously to Lane about his piano playing, and then questioning him about the cucumber sandwiches for Lady Bracknell:

> ALGERNON. And speaking of the science of Life, have you got the cucumber sandwiches cut for Lady Bracknell?
> LANE. Yes, sir. *(Hands them on a salver)*
> ALGERNON. *(Inspects them, takes two, and sits down on the sofa)* Oh! By the way, Lane . . .

This famous opening is, of course, a wonderful piece of witty writing, highly self-conscious of the theatrical conventions it revels in. But—consequently—the conventions are clear to see. The play opens with the all too familiar stage direction "Butler enters stage left and crosses; he arranges tea/answers phone/places book on desk. . . ." It is a comforting and familiar sign of upper-class respectability and theatrical conformity, establishing a tone of easy formality. The flat's precisely demarcated decorations have already indicated this. Algernon opens with casual conversation, and plenty of trivial "business": inspecting sandwiches, taking two, sitting on the sofa, and—with an expression you would never hear in Greek tragedy—casually continuing "Oh! By the way. . . ." Nothing happens "by the way" in Greek tragedy, except perhaps the murder of Oedipus's father.

The Importance of Being Earnest follows this elegant style throughout. Between the bread and butter, the handbag, and the Army Lists of the last forty years, the plot runs its course with much flopping on sofas, turning of backs, and, of course, taking of tea.

Compare Wilde's stylized world with the opening of *Hecuba* (which prompted Clare Higgins's remark). The play has two openings. First, the ghost of the murdered Polydorus appears to explain his death and to give the scene of the play. It begins with a direct address, which I will give in my own translation (1–9):

> I have come from the hiding place of the dead and the gates
>   of darkness,
> Where Hades lives apart from the gods,
> Polydorus, child of Hecuba and Priam, my father,
> Who, when danger threatened the city of Troy
> With destruction by the Greek spear, sent me out in secret,
>   in fear,
> To the home of Polymestor, a Thracian guest-friend,
> Who sows this finest portion of the plain of the Chersonese,
> Ruling by might the horse-loving people.

I have given my own rather literal translation, because any modern acting version would want to cut this monster of a sentence into easier speaking units. The one sentence stretches

over eight verses, and goes straight into a story line, and a
blunt statement of who the character is and how he comes to
be where he is. There is no indication of any movement, any
business: the play just begins, bang. And with a long, difficult
to deliver, rolling speech. Hecuba's first speech, which follows
this prologue, is no easier. She has probably been lying on the
stage through the ghost's prologue (as most modern productions have it), and begins (59–67):

> Come, children, this old woman in front of her home,
> Lift her upright, come, lift your fellow slave,
> Trojan women, take her old hand, your former queen;
> And I will lean on the bent staff of your arm,
> And push forward the slow tread of my limbs.
> Oh lightening flash of Zeus, Oh black darkness,
> Why on earth I am so stirred in the night
> By fearsome visions?

She summons the chorus (who do not appear for thirty-
five lines), as she struggles in physical discomfort, an old
woman on the cold earth. Her syntax is disrupted, her
phrases short; she cajoles, addresses the absent chorus, calls
on god and the night. She is terrified and perplexed by her
nighttime dreams. At the same time, she describes herself,
and her misery: an old woman, a queen no longer, now co-
slave with her former slaves ("child" or "children," like the
offensive use of the word "boy" for a black slave in the old
Southern states of America, is the normal Greek term to address a slave of any age). The actor who plays Hecuba is
required to start the play at a challengingly high pitch: emotionally fraught, physically struggling, in the midst of asking
for help, recognizing her changed status, and feeling terror.
There is no buildup to this emotional level; the part simply
begins at this level of intensity and continues to grow, until
Hecuba's final violent, murderous acts of revenge and pre-

dicted fate of being turned into a dog—a bestial nonhuman existence—seem cruelly inevitable.[2]

This is typical of much of Greek writing, and it puts a considerable burden on an actor used to the genteel plotting and the controlled buildup of tension in traditional theater. There are no props—in the sense of emotional supports or physical objects to busy the body with. No chairs and no telephones. The story of Deborah Warner rehearsing Fiona Shaw in the role of Electra is telling.[3] Shaw tells how for the opening weeks of rehearsal, as she tried to find her way into her characterization of Electra, she used cigarettes, and hidden caches of food on the set, to try and express the physicality of Electra. She would use the business of smoking, of finding and eating scraps, as a traditional theatrical way of expressing through external signs the psychological and physical torments of the character. It was only when Warner removed all these props that the characterization fell into place and the script became a theatrical event. Acting, stripped bare.

Both Hecuba and Electra are women on the edge who begin the play at a high pitch. But even with less overwrought characters, the same raw opening intensity exists. Antigone's first line in Sophocles' *Antigone* is an address to her sister, which, as in all theater, acts as a marker for the audience as much as an exchange between characters. But the line is almost untranslatable. Literally, it would translate as "Oh common head of very sisterhood, Ismene . . . ," or as I would prefer to translate it, "Of common kin, my very sister, Ismene." Most translations try to capture some of the feeling of this at least: "Ismene, my own sister, dear Ismene" (*World's Classics*), "Oh sister! Ismene, dear, dear sister Ismene!" (*Penguin Classics*), "My sister, my Ismene" (*Grene and Lattimore*). It is a line which immediately poses the question of what is in common between sisters (and brothers)—a problem which not only is central to the conflict of the play, but is also a nasty reminder of the special sharing of blood in the family of Oedipus. (Not enough translations keep the sense of "common," or "shared," a word repeated half a dozen times in the play at crucial junctures.) Her address suggests there are some forms of blood tie that are more important than others ("very sister"). It indicates Antigone's fierce rhetoric, her willingness to manipulate those close to her, and her passion, the passion that means that within a hundred lines of this opening affection she has dismissed her sister in a gesture that marks the irretrievable breakdown of their relationship.[4]

It is a commonplace to say of the classics that every line counts and every word matters. But the implications of this for acting are less commonly appreciated. Antigone does not simply come on, address Ismene, and move into the first expository scene (as Algernon says "Lane" and Lane says "Sir"). The address is a rich, thematically charged, difficult-to-say line. The actor playing Antigone, like Hecuba or Electra, has to hit the ground running—while knowing that the full course of the play is yet to run, with its growth of tension, its climaxes, and its violent rows. The great Shakespearian tragic roles are similarly challenging, but few other modern parts are. Finding the right level of expression is always an actor's problem: but Greek tragedy poses this problem in the most acute form, because there is *no small talk*. It is because of this that so many actors fall back on "grandeur" or "magnificence," although grandiloquence so rarely leads into the heart of any role. The first problems, then, that a modern actor faces are the lack of small talk, the lack of business, and the lack of props. Greek tragedy, for an actor, is a most exposing genre.

The lack of props does not mean that there are no items at all onstage, nor that there are no significant objects for actors to touch, hold on to, and work with. But it does mean that those few objects, those gestures, which are singled out need special care. The objects of Greek tragedy become acutely important precisely because of their rarity and the focus which they provide for the action and the actors. Brecht and Beckett, masters of modernist theater, were great readers of Greek tragedy, and their stagecraft constantly reflects this reading (though one could say that Beckett, like Pinter, made his plays out of nothing but small talk, and thus changed the very nature of theatrical language). The stripped set and obsessive focus on a particular object, a hallmark of modernist drama, is also a turn back to ancient theater.

One of the most famous stories about ancient acting concerns the actor Polus. He was already a celebrity performer when he was cast to play Sophocles' Electra. Perhaps the most moving scene in that play is when Electra takes from the disguised Orestes the urn supposed to contain her dead brother's ashes. In Sophocles' play, Electra laments over the urn with unbearable feeling. Her syntax collapses, the verse form breaks down, and eventually even the otherwise brutally unemotional Orestes collapses and confesses to her his real identity. The urn becomes the object of fixation for both of them: Orestes carries it first as his token to gain entrance to the palace to commit the revenge; Electra holds it as the last small remnant of her brother, her final hope. As Orestes questions her and builds up to his revelation, she refuses to return the urn to him. For the audience, part of the complexity of feeling here is our knowledge that she is crying over an empty urn, a mere illusion (a moment which, like Hamlet's "What's Hecuba to him?" self-reflexively exposes the strangeness of our own tears over a fiction when we watch tragedy). Polus shockingly filled the urn with the ashes of his recently dead son before he played Electra. The performance went down in Greek history as one of the most moving ever for actor and audience alike. Polus turned public theater into a form of a public ritual of mourning, and the uncanny breaking of the conditions of theatrical illusion in this of all scenes contributed to the powerful effect of Polus's tears. Yet such an anecdote totally depends on the symbolic and dramatic power with which the empty urn has been invested through the play. The lack of the equivalent of small talk with objects, no pouring of tea or fiddling with cigarette packets, makes individual objects or gestures even more intensely significant in Greek tragedy.[5]

The clarity of gesture or concentration on the object, which this economy of use imposes, is nowhere more fascinatingly in view than in Sophocles' *Philoctetes*. This play has been brought to the fore in modern theater thanks to Seamus Heaney's *The Cure at Troy*, subtitled *A Version of Sophocles' Philoctetes*, which, since its first production in Ireland and London in 1990, has rarely been out of the repertoire. There have been five productions in the United States alone since 1993, including one in New York directed by Derek Walcott.[6] In *Philoctetes*, the hero Philoctetes, left on a deserted island in excruciating agony from a poisoned foot, has only his bow to enable him to survive. It is the bow of Heracles, which never misses its target, and with it Philoctetes can get enough game to stay alive. Odysseus and Neoptolemus have come after nine years to try to persuade Philoctetes to come to Troy, where he will be cured, because an oracle has said Troy will not fall without Philoctetes and his bow. Neoptolemus agrees to try to trick Philoctetes onto their boat; then is swayed by pity at the older man's anguish; confesses the plot; and is amazed when Philoctetes refuses even so to go to Troy. It takes the appearance of the immortal hero Heracles to persuade the fiercely committed Philoctetes to abandon his hatred of the Greeks enough to find a cure at Troy. The play is much taken with trust and the breakdown of relationships through false language and concealed motivations.[7] It also focuses on the eruption of violence in response to such painful conflict, and the difficulty of seeing where decency and duty lie in such a conflicted world. It is no surprise that Heaney's version has been produced repeatedly as a response to the troubles in Northern Ireland.

The bow of Philoctetes becomes a talismanic object in the play. Once Neoptolemus has gained Philoctetes' trust, and promised him (falsely) a journey home, he broaches the subject of the bow (654–58):

> NEOPTOLEMUS. Is that really the famous bow you have
> with you?
> PHILOCTETES. Yes, this is it that I am holding.
> NEOPTOLEMUS. And may I look at it in close detail,
> And hold it and revere as a god?
> PHILOCTETES. You may, my child . . .

Philoctetes explains that because Neoptolemus has so helped him and is his savior, he alone can touch the bow. To touch the bow becomes a gesture that indicates a special bond of trust between the two men. Indeed, when Philoctetes is collapsing into a fit because of his poisoned foot, he gives Neoptolemus the bow to hold and protect against any Greek who should come after him. Neoptolemus has the bow—one half of his mission—but he is wrung out by the pity he feels for Philoctetes. When the hero comes to, he tells him of the plot to deceive him—but nonetheless refuses to return the bow. "Duty and expedience require me to obey those in authority." Philoctetes, however, would rather die in solitary anguish than do anything to help his enemies who deserted him on the island. Neoptolemus, unable to change Philoctetes' mind, leaves him—only to return shortly, pursued by a desperate Odysseus, to give back the bow. It is this gesture—an action, not words—which starts to rebuild the relationship between the two men, wrecked by Neoptolemus's deceit and Philoctetes' intransigence.

Who holds the bow, who hands it to whom, who withholds the bow, becomes a potent symbol; the bow is the object around which the patterns of trust and power revolve. This is a particularly powerful example of how any object can be used in drama of any period. It makes not only the object itself hugely significant for the action of the play, but also each gesture of handling it. In a play which so often talks about the relation between words and action, that is, between deceitful, powerful language, and the hard reality of things and deeds, the bow becomes the prime dramatic focus.

For actors, this use of the bow is a guide through the intense physicality of this drama. It provides a material aim for Neoptolemus and an external sign of the shifting relationships of power and trust. Yet in Sophocles there is none of the clomping symbolism and heavy-handed dialogue you get, for example, with Wagner's magic weapons. The bow is introduced early on, but then Neoptolemus sidles round the topic over fully five hundred lines of building a relationship with Philoctetes. It becomes invested with significance at key moments of the action because of the way the characters are interacting, and because it gets used as an object of exchange in a play about the collapse of relations of exchange. For an actor, the bow is not like a chair or a telephone, a prop that helps get through a scene by providing a set of easy physical actions to structure movement across the stage. Rather, every time the bow is touched, talked of, or passed from hand to hand, it provides an immediate and intense charge for the scene. It is the opposite of easy and familiar physical action, and because of this, every moment of such focus needs great care onstage, not to become either overblown or passed over.[8]

Objects like Philoctetes' bow, which are freighted with such significance, are used with particular power at moments of dramatic climax. So, Cassandra at the end of her grueling scene of prophecy in Aeschylus's *Agamemnon*, as she realizes that she has persuaded no one of the fate of the king, and that she too is progressing helplessly to her own death, begins her long exit to the house by ripping off her prophetic headdress and robes and throwing them to the ground. Her gift of foresight has made no difference, and she marks the uselessness of her knowledge by violently discarding the insignia of her role. This was marvelously visualized in Katie Mitchell's

10 Lilo Bauer as Cassandra in Katie Mitchell's *Oresteia*, veiled and delivering her wild prophecies.

production of the *Oresteia* at the National Theatre in London in 1999 (fig. 10).[9] When Cassandra ripped off her bridal veils (through which she had screamed her prophecies), she revealed her naked breasts covered in bite marks, and caked blood on her body. The violence she had experienced was shockingly and suddenly evident. Ajax, in Sophocles' *Ajax*, kills himself alone onstage (the chorus, uniquely, has been removed from the stage): he begins his final speech with nine lines about the sword he will use to kill himself, as he fixes it in the ground, ready to fall on. It was a gift from the Trojan

Hector, his hated enemy. The sword symbolizes how twisted relations of duty and hatred can become, and how for Ajax now there is no action he can take to respond to the world, except to destroy himself. The first word of the speech is *ho sphageus*, "The sword/slayer." The ancient actor Timotheus became so famous for playing this scene that he was known as "The Sword." It gives a vivid reminder of how the actor's relation to an object can become the keynote of a famous performance.[10]

There is a wonderful example of how the body itself can become such an object of intense focus in the work of Peter Stein, the celebrated German director.[11] When Orestes confronts Clytemnestra in the *Libation Bearers*, the middle play of the *Oresteia*, Clytemnestra says, "Pity the breast at which you suckled, my child," and this plea prompts Orestes' famous moment of tragic doubt: "Pylades, what should I do? Should decency stop me from killing my mother?" (fig. 11). In Stein's early 1980s production, Clytemnestra (Edith Clever), as she

11 "Pity the breast at which you suckled, my child": Clytemnestra (Edith Clever) stops Orestes in his tracks in Peter Stein's *Oresteia*.

said her line, removed her naked breast from her costume, and Orestes' drawn sword was pressed hard against it. As she demanded respect, she moved toward him, and her breast, wielded like a weapon, moved Orestes backward. As his resolve hardened, however, he moved her toward the house, with his sword still pushing into the vulnerable flesh. Throughout the scene, Orestes' sword remained pressed hard against her skin. The mother's breast, suddenly and with immense physical and symbolic impact, became the pivot of the scene. Stein revealed brilliantly the physical potential of Aeschylus's script.

I can think of very few scenes in Greek tragedy, however, which come even close to the standard modern use of the physical and verbal props in naturalistic contemporary theater. Perhaps the best example is the opening scene of Euripides' *Ion*, where Ion begins the play as a temple servant, sweeping the steps of the temple and shooing away the birds. The broom he carries and uses is explicitly marked out as an everyday object, just as the sweeping is a daily event. But even here, Ion intersperses his cleaning with a hymn to the god, enacting a ritual prayer as he goes about his business. Casual objects, gestures, or words are few and far between in tragedy. As with Shakespearian theater, learning to use the stage space and one's body without tea or telephones is one of the most productive challenges of ancient tragedy for a modern actor.

Bizarrely, even silence is affected by the difference between ancient and modern theater. In modern drama, silence is, as it were, the default mode. That is, when the butler Lane enters stage left and crosses stage right, he does so in silence (and that is the convention). Many plays begin in silence. Actors have plenty of scenes where they busy themselves around a room in silence before another character comes on to initiate dialogue (papers to sort, books to shelve, cushions to arrange). The opposite is true in Greek tragedy. Silence is a marked mode. Plays begin with words, and the only time that silence is heard is for a specific and emphatic point. Silence is always palpable in

Greek tragedy (as, say, in Pinter). The fact that Cassandra does not speak when addressed by Clytemnestra in the *Agamemnon* is commented on by all the other figures onstage and full of significance. It is a sign of her resistance—and her special relation to language and knowledge. When Ajax lies in his tent silent, it is clear to the other characters he is contemplating something terrible. Silence is a deliberate breaking of the exchange of communication, and is an aggressive gesture. Tragedy's world of articulate horror makes silence the last resort: when Jocasta in *Oedipus the King* exits in silence (as too does Deianeira in the *Women of Trachis*), it is in order to kill herself in horror at what she has done. "I fear evil will burst forth from her silence," comment the terrified chorus. Most modern actors (and audiences) are accustomed to the comfort of silence: in Greek tragedy, silence is a frightening, dumbstruck refusal to speak.[12]

]]] [[[

Many productions of Greek tragedy in contemporary theaters, misled by the formal debates and the absence of dramatic bustle, fall back on lack of movement as a response to these scripts. But tragedy is also intensely physical, it uses space with deep sophistication (as we have seen), and demands a heightened awareness of the importance of physical gesture, the symbolic power of objects, the fragility of the body, the displays of power and persuasion. Tragedy exposes the actor by removing the props of modern theater, but, as generations of great actors have shown, these plays also offer extraordinary opportunities to display a brilliance unencumbered by the clutter and fussing of bourgeois drama.

Speaking the Language of Tragedy

So, exposed onstage, without the props of chairs and telephone, without the comfort zones of easy silence or casual words, how does the actor speak? There are three particular types of speech that need special attention. First, what is known as *stichomythia*—that is, the formal exchange of single lines between two actors, or between actor and chorus; second, the messenger speech; third, the so-called *rhesis*, the extended, rhetorical speech. Each brings with it a special set of difficulties for the modern actor.

Dialogue

Stichomythia is one of the hallmarks of tragedy to a modern mind. The formality of the exchange of single lines is easily parodied. The poet and classical scholar A. E. Housman (star of Tom Stoppard's *The Invention of Love*) wickedly caught the hilarity of bad translation and the apparent lumpiness of such dramatic technique in his "Fragment of a Greek Tragedy":

CHORUS. To learn your name would not displease me
      much.
ALCMAEON. Not all that men desire do they obtain.
CHORUS. Might I then hear at what your presence shoots?
ALCMAEON. A shepherd's questioned mouth informed me
      that—
CHORUS. What? For I do not know what you will say.
ALCMAEON. Nor will you ever, if you interrupt.
CHORUS. Proceed and I will hold my speechless tongue.

I particularly like the acid precision of the chorus's intervention "What? For I do not know what you will say," but the whole dialogue recalls rather too sharply for comfort a good number of painfully clumsy stagings of tragedy.

This parody would suggest that stichomythia is where we will find small talk in tragedy—the necessary exchange of information, the simple questions of who are you and where are you from, the background to the heated debates to come.

But this is a misleading impression. Just as Antigone's opening address to Ismene comes heavily laden with meaning and import, so even the conversations between chorus and an arriving messenger can challenge an audience with swirls of meaning. My favorite example is in *Oedipus the King*, though we will need a little Greek to help us appreciate the power of Sophocles' writing. Jocasta has just prayed to Apollo for release (a dreadful irony in itself, granted how quickly her "release" is to come), and right on cue, as if in answer to the prayer, the messenger arrives from Corinth with the news of the death of the king there, Oedipus's apparent father. His message leads to the unraveling of everything. He comes in and says (924–26), "May I learn from you, strangers, where the house of Oedipus the king is? In particular, tell me if you know where he himself is." This looks like as bland an utterance as there could be. But in Greek the language has been turned in a wholly bizarre way so that the three lines end with a weird jingle: *mathoim' hopou/Oidipou/katisth' hopou*—"May I learn where?/Oedipus/Do you know where?" Consequently, we hear in the simple questions a transfixing pun: *Oedipus* means "*know where?*" The name of the king resounds with the problem that has destroyed him: not knowing where he is or where he comes from. The chorus reply, "This is his house. He is inside. This is his wife and mother of his children." In the half beat of a breath between the words "mother" and "of his children," the audience hear an equally revealing and horrific reply: "This is his wife and mother." When an actor thinks that a line in a script of a tragedy is mere small talk, it is almost certain that the line has not been understood.

Stichomythia is a flexible and precise tool of communication, which has a special role in tragedy. For stichomythia is a marvelously economical way of dramatizing the breakdown of communication into conflicting positions. Tragedy is a genre of conflict: not only conflict between people or between ideas, but also conflict about what words mean. Characters repeatedly use the same words in different senses. They argue over what words to use, and they use them as weapons against each other. Stichomythia is the prime medium of this violent war of words. Let me give one example first from Sophocles' *Philoctetes* which shows the brilliant economy of this style of writing. Odysseus is persuading Neoptolemus to join in the plot to capture Philoctetes. "The tongue," he says, rules all" (100–109):

NEOPTOLEMUS. What then are you telling me to do except tell lies.

ODYSSEUS. I am telling you to catch Philoctetes with a trick.

NEOPTOLEMUS. Why must I take him by a trick and not by persuasion?

ODYSSEUS. He will never be persuaded. And force is no use.

NEOPTOLEMUS. Does he have such a terrible power of strength?

ODYSSEUS. Inescapable arrows which are lethal.

NEOPTOLEMUS. Isn't it rash even to have contact with him, then?

ODYSSEUS. Yes, unless you catch him, that is, by a trick, as I say.

NEOPTOLEMUS. Do you not actually think it disgraceful to tell lies?

ODYSSEUS. Not if the lie brings safety at least.

In ten lines, a complex exchange unfurls. First, Neoptolemus rejects Odysseus's invitation with the dismissal that for all the general talk about the tongue and power, it is just the disgraceful act of lying that is being asked for. Odysseus, however, tries to redefine "lies" as "a trick," a less morally charged alternative. In response, Neoptolemus redefines his own position: why not persuasion? Surely Philoctetes would listen to their argument if it is good and just. No, says, Odysseus (rightly as it turns out). Philoctetes is beyond persuasion. What is more, he adds, closing off another line of argument for the young Neoptolemus, force, the opposite of persuasion, is not going to succeed either. So, wonders Neoptolemus, how could any contact be wise? That, says Odysseus, is exactly why a trick is necessary. Neoptolemus's defence has been turned by Odysseus's carefully positioned argument. So Neoptolemus tries another tack. Can there really be any situation where telling lies is moral? Of course, retorts Odysseus, when a lie brings salvation: this is the hero, after all, who escapes from the Cyclops' cave only by a lie and a trick. Another line of defence for Neoptolemus has been breached.

The conversation has a clear logic, as the audience watches the older and more experienced power broker manipulate the younger more idealistic figure into doing what he wants. Each word which Neoptolemus takes up to express his unwillingness to behave in a disreputable manner—lies, disgrace, persuasion—is delicately shifted by Odysseus into a different moral register—trick, safety, force. In a mere ten lines, the dialogue shifts direction round and round about as Neoptolemus is gradually, unwillingly, reeled in to the plot.

This is a calm and controlled discussion from the opening minutes of a play. But despite that, it is not just "establishing dialogue." It is in itself a small drama of persuasion, which opens immediately into the major dramatic themes of the play. It requires careful and precise acting, that inhabits the language and its sinuousness, to communicate the careful precision of its writing (even in translation). Often stichomythia expresses a more aggressive breakdown into opposition of characters in conflict. In Sophocles, indeed, stichomythia often ends with mutual accusations of madness or mutual accusations of hatred: Haemon screaming at Creon in *Antigone*; Menelaus snobbishly insulting Teucer in *Ajax*. But here too the depth, precision, and density of the language of the exchanges put considerable demands on the actor's ability to express both emotion and articulacy. This is the very nub of stichomythia for the actor. To be able to communicate powerful emotions within the short space of a dense, articulate, single verse; and to communicate the flow of conflicting emotions through so formal a style of verse exchange. In all senses, stichomythia is designed to make conflicting emotions articulate. It anatomizes argument.

This can be achieved both in the more naturalistic style of modern productions such as those of Deborah Warner or Katie Mitchell, and in the more stylized productions of Ariane Mnouchkine or Peter Hall. The Hall/Harrison *Oresteia* made the exchange of stichomythia absolutely formalized and antirealist by slowing down the delivery and putting a crash of music between each line. This put a great deal of weight on the semantic significance of each line, as the argument unfurled. But for both realist and stylized productions, the challenge of stichomythia remains the same for actor and director alike.

The Messenger Speech

The messenger speech is just as much a familiar icon of Greek tragedy as stichomythia, but brings quite different concerns to the fore. The standard image is hard to shake when it comes to the messenger speech. It goes like this: almost all violence in tragedy happens offstage; it is reported by a messenger, who enters, tells the audience what has happened in lurid detail, and then goes off. It is a great opportunity for a show-stealing speech, like Mercutio's Queen Mab in *Romeo and Juliet*. But that is all.

One minute with the scripts of Sophocles will show how naïve this standard image is. In *Electra*, the "messenger" is actually the Tutor, who tells a wholly false tale about the death of Orestes as part of the plot of deception. The audience watches a master rhetorician spin a set of lies—while being hooked into the story. The scene becomes a transfixing reflection on the deceptive lures of fiction. Later, as the murder actually takes place, it is Electra's violent commentary that takes us through the action.

In *Oedipus the King*, there are three messengers: the first from Corinth, as we have just seen, always seems to say more than he means to, and unwittingly reveals the full horror of the family history to Jocasta; the second, the herdsman, wishes to say nothing, and is forced into revealing the family saga to Oedipus himself; the third, from inside the house, tells of Jocasta's hanging and Oedipus's blinding. He cannot bear to say what he has seen (though he does). Three men, who, in this play of ironic revelation, reveal the truth through three different gestures of unwillingness.

In *Women of Trachis*, the news of Heracles' anguish is brought by his son Hyllas, and delivered to his mother, who kills herself because of it. Far from the objective reportage of events, this is a story that is fully part of violence within the family (and which the messenger will come deeply to regret). There is no messenger in *Philoctetes*, though Odysseus, in order to further the deception of Philoctetes, does send in a false Merchant with a lying tale of a Greek mission to chase down Philoctetes. In short, there is a huge variety in the use of the messenger, variety in the relationship between the messenger and the action, in the type of story told, in the styles of delivery.

What this variety implies is that the regular cliché of a center-stage address to the audience (sometimes with acting out of the violent scenes described) is only one—and one not very imaginative—solution to the problem of an extended storytelling scene within tragedy. The messenger scene is a crucial part of tragedy's obsession with narrative and interpretation, and with the response to violence and horror. It needs a performance style that integrates the scene into the play as a whole—and this requires an understanding of the specifics of each play's treatment of the convention.

Let me give two examples of how understanding the specific dynamics of the messenger's role in the play is essential to a staging. The two messengers in the *Bacchae* reflect the double responses to the god, Dionysus, who is described in the play as "most gentle and most terrible for humans." The first, a herdsman, comes to tell of the miraculous scene of the women on the mountain, where milk and wine flow from the soil, and the women suckle wild animals. It is an awestruck response to the epiphanic power of the god, and is delivered significantly between Pentheus's attempt to imprison Dionysus, and the king's own fateful trip to the mountains. The messenger has to find a way of telling the miraculous things he has seen to a disbelieving and violently angry master. His wonder exacerbates the king's violent resolve against the Bacchants. The second messenger, by contrast, tells of the king's death in shock and terror at the violence the god has caused. He is horrified at the chorus's delighted response to his news. His grim news excites their ecstatic madness. Neither man, in short, simply delivers a message. Both have to deal with a specific audience and a specific response to their news. Both scenes stage conflicting responses to the god. In this way, both men are fully part of the play's dramatization of the question of how to comprehend Dionysus.

The messenger in the *Agamemnon*, however, my second example, is an outrider of the returning king. Rather than offer any simple triumphalist account of the fall of Troy and the return of the military hero, he tells an increasingly miserable tale. He opens with prayers of thanks for his return and announces the victory, but as the scene progresses he gives a somewhat depressing account of the grimness of the siege, and ends with the news of the awful storm that has wrecked the fleet on its way home. A descent into despondency is a repeated move in the trilogy, but here it also acts as an ominous

preparation for the arrival of the king, and a darkly revision-
ist account of the epic triumph over the Trojans. His news is
responded to with different excitement by the chorus and by
Clytemnestra. The messenger in turn quite fails to understand the chorus's veiled hints about the problems at home,
just as he fails to realize that the message he will take from
Clytemnestra back to the king is part of her deceitful plot
against him. There is a range of messages being sent here—
and this is part of the *Oresteia*'s fascination with the power
and danger of language in action.

As these scenes from the *Bacchae* and the *Oresteia* vividly
demonstrate, a messenger may be anonymous, but he always
has a specific and unique role in each play. This is partly a
question of character: the gruff soldier, the awestruck ob-
server of the Bacchants. Each messenger tells his own story.
What's more, there is always an audience onstage for the messenger, and this relationship between messenger and audience
changes the rhetorical strategies of the speech. But perhaps
the hardest element of the messenger speech to appreciate is
the way in which the playwrights manipulate the formal nature of the scene, and make the messenger part of themes
of the drama. It is not by chance that the messenger of the
Agamemnon brings a confusing message of good and bad news
in a trilogy obsessed with how language is used, and with the
transition from dark to light, and from conflict to order. This
all helps us see why the standard image of the messenger of
Greek tragedy is so insufficient. It is the job of the actor and
director to get away from those misleading clichés.

The Formal Speech

Perhaps the hardest speeches of all for a modern actor to feel
at home with are the long set speeches, which characterize
so much of Greek tragedy. The formal political speech—like
Oedipus's opening address to the people of Thebes in *Oedipus*

the King, or Creon's speech on taking up power in Sophocles'
Antigone—is a familiar genre and brings no special surprises.
So, too, the long arias of despair or lamentation—Oedipus's
blind entrance, Hecuba's mourning over Astyanax in the
Trojan Women—while fiendishly difficult to deliver well, are
recognizably the ancestors of the Renaissance rhetoric of
grief, which are standards of the classical actor's repertoire.
What are more problematic in Greek tragedy are the long argumentative speeches, which make up the scenes of debate,
or the *agon*, as it is known. When Medea argues with Jason
in *Medea*, or Hippolytus with Theseus in *Hippolytus*, or Antigone with Creon in *Antigone*, we see fierce arguments between intimately related people on matters of deep personal
concern. Yet these arguments seem to turn all too quickly
into abstract cases or philosophical positions, which seem far
removed from any modern expectation of how a husband and
wife, son and father, uncle and niece, would enter into violent conflict.[13]

Take Hippolytus in Euripides' *Hippolytus*, a play that gave
rise to Racine's *Phèdre* and many other modern versions. He
is accused by his father of raping his stepmother. She has left
a letter accusing him of this foul crime, before hanging herself. His speech of defence begins with words that sound extraordinary to a modern ear (983–93):

> Father, the strength and composition of your mind is
> Awesome. But the matter, for all the fine arguments,
> If someone were to unfold it, is not fine.
> I am unsophisticated at giving speeches to the mob.
> I am more skilled before a few men of my own age.
> This too has its place. For those who are poor amongst the
>   wise,
> Are more cultured at speaking in front of the mob.
> But I must, as the circumstances have arisen,
> Give free rein to my tongue. First, I will begin my speech

From the point you first attacked me, to destroy me
Without my speaking in reply. . . .

The speech is full of the markers of a formal legal wrangling. Rather than as a son before his father, he speaks as if he were before a popular court (including the standard trope that he is "unaccustomed to such public speaking"). How should a modern actor face such a speech? How can such rhetoric be understood in such familial turmoil?

There are two separate but interrelated answers to this question, one specific to this play, and one more general to tragedy. The specifics concern the play's plot and thematic focus. Hippolytus has taken an oath not to reveal that Phaedra actually desired him (and that he rejected the nurse's advances on her behalf). The formal rhetoric conceals an immense struggle within him. Will he reveal the truth which could save himself—but break his solemn oath? When he says "if someone were to unfold it," and "I must as the circumstances have arisen give free rein to my tongue," he is hinting to the audience that he will speak out. But he does not. The formal legal language is a blind, concealing the truth and Hippolytus's own emotional upset.[14]

But this is not just any legal language. Hippolytus is also representing himself as a nasty young aristocrat. In Athens, only a right-wing opponent of democracy would simply call the people "the mob." When he says he is more used to speaking to a few young men of his own age, he is indicating his elitist, antidemocratic, politically dodgy affiliations. The audience thus are thrown into a typically Euripidean complexity of emotions: they watch the young man sympathetically but self-destructively hold on to his principles and not break his oath; at the same time, they have to listen to his posturing as an offensive right-wing aristocrat.

This is not just a straight speech of defence. The speech is the desperate performance of a particular young man caught in a horrific double bind, a speech that twists the audience's emotions in conflicting directions. It is fully part of the play's dramatic fascination with how words work, what purity is, and how humans become sucked into tragedy by their own desires and misprisions.

So we can see how the general-sounding rhetoric of this speech is actually located precisely in the character and action of the moment. But there is a second, more general answer to how the rhetoric of this scene works, for which we need to turn to the intellectual and social world of fifth-century Athens. It will help us understand further how the rhetoric of tragedy speaks to the ancient city and to us today.

Democracy is a system that depends on public displays of speech-making.[15] The Assembly and the law courts were the main routes to power in the city, and both required a citizen to speak for himself in public. Any citizen could find himself as part of the Council, the executive arm of government, whose five hundred members were elected by lot each year, and thus having to take part in public debate. In the Assembly, state policy was made. Deciding whether to go to war or what economic policy to follow was debated by the citizens and voted on: evaluating argument, as well as making arguments, was a crucial aspect of civic duty. It could be a life-or-death matter for individuals in the court, or for the state in the discussions in the Assembly. It is perhaps no surprise that the Athenians of the fifth century were obsessed with the power of speech. Rhetoric, the formal study of speech-making, was invented as a discipline at this time. Rhetoric promised to train the speaker to win arguments, or even to make the weaker argument the stronger. This was not just a good advertising slogan for the professional rhetorician trying to sell his art. It threatened the very heart of the democratic constitution. If the weaker argument became the winning case, what happened to foreign policy? What happened to you in court if your opponent was trained and you were not? The threat and power of language was an endemic concern of fifth-century Athens.

This is one crucial element of background to a speech like Hippolytus's self-defence. We are watching a man trained in rhetoric, unable to make it work for him: this speech of self-defence is actually a sign of the wreckage of Hippolytus's self. The failure of rhetoric speaks to society's worries and its politics.

But there is another aspect which is equally important. In the modern West, there is a very strong contrast between public and private life. The bourgeois home is a castle, protected by law and defended by society's moralists. Privacy is a privileged value of modern culture. Politics, by contrast, is conducted in the public sphere, and the public sphere has its own expectations and styles of self-presentation. The division between the public and the private is strongly articulated, and it is in the private where the truth of the person is located: in private, a person can be herself, be sincere, and find her most fulfilling relationships (or so the story goes). To say that "the personal is political" is a polemical attempt to redraw the boundaries to bring the politics of feminism into the household. It is a provocation that depends on the normal and expected opposition of the personal and the political.

In ancient Greece, this modern bourgeois opposition of public and private would seem quite baffling. Democracy depends on all its citizens contributing to the city, and each man's life is part of the city. Aristotle can argue that suicide is wrong because each person belongs to the city: what we might see as a personal act of despair is seen as a civic event, and its morality judged as such. Socrates can wander up to someone in the street and berate him for being flabby, because he will be fighting for the state, and such poor conditioning will threaten his colleagues and the city's welfare. His naked body is public property. (Fat is a political issue.) Any citizen could find himself in court and his domestic life put under scrutiny in front of a large jury of the people, even—especially—in a financial case. In Athens, democracy made every aspect of a citizen's life part of the public life of the city. The opposition of public and private life just doesn't work for Greek tragedy.

This helps explain why Hippolytus speaks the way he does. It is not a surprise that he talks as if he were before a popular jury. Nor is there is a private world of chat between father and son that is being hidden or ignored. Hippolytus speaks as if he were before the people because democratic life is constantly lived as if it were before the people—and much of it actually was so lived. The links between a family's turmoil and political principles were evident, important, and to be explored. The row between Haemon and Creon in Sophocles' *Antigone* is between a son and a father about the boy's fiancée; it will end up with the boy threatening his father and killing himself over the body of the girl. The argument they have is conducted in terms of political principle and how the city should be ruled. This continuity between the intimacy of the family and the theory of political power is *typical*.

Yet it is precisely this sort of language that causes the modern actor problems, especially when the actor has been trained to discover a private intimacy and internalized feeling as the most powerfully expressive form of acting. The first step must be to recognize that the public, political argument is a normal and expected form of self-representation or self-expression in tragedy. The production of *Iphigeneia at Aulis* by Katie Mitchell (in 2004 in London) was particularly adept at this. This is a play where a girl, a daughter, is to be sacrificed for the sake of the military expedition. The play brilliantly captured how the abstract political arguments about benefit and national duty led to personal anguish; and also, with the daughter's ready willingness to die, how such arguments could be absorbed by the victims—with, in this case, a heart-breaking irony of innocence. Similarly, in Jonathan Kent's *Hecuba*, Odysseus's cynical but sincere arguments about why Hecuba's daughter

has to die for the morale of the troops, and Agamemnon's eva-
sive decision to wash his hands of Hecuba's desire for revenge,
superbly evoked men's distorted and distorting, self-serving
arguments under the conditions of war. It is not by chance that
both of these plays, produced in the aftermath of the second
invasion of Iraq, focused on the manipulative and desperate
way powerful figures behave in war. The contemporary political situation gave the audience a ready framework of comprehension and a sharp sense of relevance.

It is extraordinary how often a production of Greek
tragedy—in realistic or stylized mode—assumes that the
speech-making requires the abstract pomposity and formal
self-presentation of a political address. Men barking across
the stage at each other. As Zoë Wanamaker, fresh from her
performance as Electra, said, "I had been intimidated by
Greek tragedy basically because I felt it was masks and people
speaking in funny voices"—a feeling that neatly punctures
this haranguing style of performance.[16] This manner of acting—which I too find relentlessly unengaging—stems from a
misunderstanding based on the modern expectations of the
difference between public and private worlds (of feeling, language, self-presentation). The heroes and heroines of Greek
tragedy live *all* their life in the glare of the scrutiny of the
city: their intimacy, their family arguments, are all acted
out on this same stage. Even when a woman cries inside the
house, she is heard on the outside. The marital row of Jason
and Medea is enacted in front of the chorus and outside the
house. The public stage is the place of true feeling, passionate and intimate argument, and engagement with the citizen's
life in the city. It is a space of expression that is rich, varied,
and ready for the actor's creative exploration.

The scripts of ancient tragedy are especially hard to penetrate for a modern actor: these three formal aspects—stichomythia, messenger speeches, and the speech-making of the
agon—can be intimidating or alienating, and certainly can

lead to some dull, pompous, and annoying acting. What I hope to have shown, however, is that when these formal aspects are properly understood, they open up a world of subtle flexibility and expressive richness, a resource an actor can trust. As with Shakespeare's iambic pentameter, *form* can be a barrier to the inexperienced actor, but it can also become an unparalleled source of theatrical power.

Characterization

The modern actor within the realist Western tradition is trained when working with a part to develop a character, to think through a character's history—the back story—and to explore the psychological depths and motivation for each action. Greek tragedy can make this very difficult. The texts can seem unshakably bland—there are no physical habits or verbal mannerisms to build a portrait from; there are barely any roles for "character actors"; there are only a few indications through costume or language of the standard modern background of class, education, family history. Greek tragedy is the opposite end of the spectrum from a Dickens novel. This can leave an actor feeling unanchored.

The scholarly response to this is worth knowing, though in all probability it will only occasionally help a performer.[17] In the ancient world, the argument runs, there is a quite different interest in character from today. When ancient philosophers or novelists talk about character, they are interested not so much in individualism for its own sake, but in general types (much as classical statues are never warts-and-all portraits, but idealized images). So, in most forms of Greek literature, there is no attempt to describe a "character" in the way that Thackeray, for example, lovingly draws the specific and individual traits of Becky Sharpe in *Vanity Fair*, nor are there those telltale marks of oddity that Dickens revels in—the verbal mannerism, the bizarre behavior, the weird item of dress.

Rather we get a work like Theophrastus's *Characters*. Theophrastus was a fourth-century philosopher, one of the successors of Aristotle; his book *Characters* is a collection of short prose sketches. There we meet "The Superstitious Man," or "The Boorish Man"—and a whole host of other types. In each case, we are presented with a set of characteristic behaviors of such and such a fellow: So the Superstitious Man is "someone who if a cat crosses his path, will not proceed on his way until someone else has gone by, or he has thrown three stones across the street" (some superstitions have a very long history). The Boorish Man when he sits down will lift his robe too high and reveal his naked genitals (and some sorts of masculine vulgarity have a long history too . . .). In tragedy, therefore, the argument continues, there is a tendency to represent ideal types or to question ideal types. Agamemnon is a king, and the marks of his behavior are highlighted insofar as they illumine the role of a good or bad king. Creon is a ruler, and, as he himself says, "It is difficult to find out completely about the soul, the disposition, and the judgment of any man, until you have seen him exercised in the business of rule and law-giving" (*Ant* 175–77). It is through his role as ruler, not through any individual psychodynamics of personality, that we evaluate and understand Creon as a figure.

This argument is broadly convincing, if superficial, in the form I have so far expressed it. We will see how much this position needs to be nuanced as we progress. But for the moment one conclusion might be that for those who see Greek tragedy as a resolutely unrealistic theatrical genre (as Ariane Mnouchkine and Peter Hall, among many others, insist), the representation of figures onstage as types goes hand in hand with a stylized form of acting and stylized staging.

There are some considerable advantages to this concept of tragedy too. In the so-called Carpet Scene of Aeschylus's *Agamemnon*, Clytemnestra spreads the blood-red tapestries on the floor before the door of the palace and asks Agamemnon to tread across them into the house. It is, of course, a highly symbolic gesture—to march as if in blood to the house; to trample on fine things; to destroy the house's wealth; to be shown to act in such a way before the people. (One of Katie Mitchell's most stunning moments in her 1999 *Oresteia* was to have this carpet made out of the little red dresses of the sacrificed Iphigeneia.) Critics have regularly asked why Agamemnon does step onto the tapestries, since he has been quite clear, when Clytemnestra first suggests it, that such an act is wrong, barbaric, and sacrilegious.

Approaching the scene in terms of modern "hunt the motivation" has proven a deeply unsatisfactory enterprise. For Fraenkel, the great German scholar writing in 1950, it was because Agamemnon is a "gentleman" and could not politely refuse his wife. For Denniston and Page, English scholars writing a little later, it was because he was arrogant and vain, and wanted to indulge himself in such a lavish spectacle all along.[18] There is not a word in the script to support either interpretation. What is in the text is Clytemnestra's performance of persuasion, culminating in the demand "Be persuaded! Willingly yield power here to me!" It is the persuasion of the king by a woman, his yielding of masculine authority, that is being dramatized—and any internal psychological life of the king is secondary to this display. Here is a good example of how the ancient idea of "character" lets us see the heart of the action, where a modern idea of psychological motivation conceals what really matters.

Character may not be formed according to modern, psychological lines, then, but this does not mean that there is no interest in the internal life of the figures onstage. Far from it. A play like Sophocles' *Ajax* has every character wonder about the psychological state of the hero: is he mad or sane? Will he kill himself or not? Was he a great man or a dangerous psychopath? Euripides' *Medea* opens with the nurse terrified about Medea's intentions, and the audience watches transfixed as Medea herself struggles with her conflicting desires in the famous monologue where she eventually does decide to kill her children. Every character onstage asks the question of what Medea wants—and so too does the audience. It would be crass to suggest that Greek tragedy was not fascinated by the motivation, disposition, and internal struggles of its great heroes and heroines. And this recognition opens the way for the great realist productions such as those of Deborah Warner, or Katie Mitchell.

To explore the creative tension between these two ways of looking at character—the stylized, generalizing form versus the psychologically fraught—let us look first at motivation. We can see a fascinating difference between Aeschylus, Sophocles, and Euripides here if we look at their representations of Orestes. In Aeschylus's *Oresteia*, Orestes explains explicitly how he has come to the point of matricide. He describes the oracle of Apollo, the terrible punishments with which he is threatened if he does not undertake the revenge. He adds (298–304):

> Even if I did not obey, the deed must be done.
> Many desires come together in one act:
> The commands of god, great grief for my father;
> In addition, lack of money oppresses me.
> Nor should the most famous citizens,
> Destroyers of Troy with a noble spirit,
> Be slaves in this way to two women.

His motivations are itemized: grief; the need for material resources (this is typical of the Greek sense of the economics of the household, even if it is to the modern mind a deeply distasteful reason for killing one's mother!); a political objective of freedom. This list of motivations is followed by the great mourning song, sung by the avengers and the chorus, to summon the help of the dead father. It would seem that the revenge is to proceed on the course here laid out. But at the sticking point, Orestes hesitates. After the murder, he will flee the stage in mental disarray. It might seem that there has been a sea change in the character, and that we could read into his dry analysis of motivation a forceful repression of anxiety. But Orestes' hesitation in front of his mother is not necessarily a sign of mental torment: he asks for moral authorization, and gets it (and never afterward doubts the rightness of what he has done). When he flees the stage, it is because he is pursued by his mother's Furies, the dog-like figures of revenge. His is not so much a mental breakdown as a threatened punishment by divine powers. He will go on to defend himself in the courtroom in Athens.

In Aeschylus's Orestes, then, motivation is explicit and, in the case of his madness, external. This would seem to suggest that it is not necessary to seek to fill in a host of complex psychological mechanisms behind the action and words. In the *Oresteia*, matricide has political, social, and theological implications, but it is not a source of internalized anguish. One can see why this trilogy particularly appealed to Mnouchkine, for whom "psychological drama is not art," or to Hall, with his fascination with the mask.

In Sophocles' *Electra*, Orestes appears only in the first and last scenes. He barely mentions the oracle. The question he asked the god, he tells us (32–34), is "How should I take revenge on the killers of my father?" He asks "how" not "if." For him, there is no question as to whether the act is right, and there is no question throughout of hesitating. His final exit to kill Aegisthus is apparently untroubled. There is no sign of madness or pursuit by the Furies. And here, as we have seen, is where the questions start to rise. The silence of Orestes and the play's silence about the Furies leave the audience with a distinct unease. Can a matricide have no consequences? What have hate and bitterness done to Electra and Orestes? Should we look to find the Furies in Electra's soul?[19]

The play's silences prompt a wonder about motivation—about the "soul, disposition, and judgment" of the avenging brother and sister. Sophocles' *Electra* is set in creative tension with Aeschylus's *Oresteia*, and the very different representation of Orestes also raises a different type of question about the internal life of its leading characters. Orestes' grimness of determination, particularly when it is juxtaposed to Electra's excessive outpouring of feeling, raises the profound problem of the relation between emotions and ethics, the role of violent feelings in the pursuit of justice. Motivation itself is part of the play's deepest concerns.

In Euripides' *Electra*, Orestes appears in disguise; he feels the need to scout out the land before undertaking any revenge at all. He questions his self-dramatizing sister, and misunderstands her answers. He tries not to be recognized at all. When the Old Man forces him into the open, it is far from clear that he wants to complete the matricide. Electra develops the plot for it, and pushes him toward the deed. Here is part of the dialogue, as the queen is seen approaching the farmer's cottage, and the ambush (968–73):

ORESTES. What on earth are we to do? Will we kill mother?

ELECTRA. Surely pity hasn't got you, when you see mother's body?

ORESTES. Ah!
How can I kill the woman who bore me and raised me?

ELECTRA. Just as she killed yours and my father.

ORESTES. Apollo, your oracle was really stupid.

ELECTRA. When Apollo is off-beam, who is wise?

ORESTES. His oracle said to kill mother, which is wrong.

This dialogue replays the scene from the *Oresteia* in ironic anticipation. Will Orestes hesitate when he sees his mother's body? Will he seek divine authority? Electra dismisses the possibility of doubt, but Orestes is more than doubtful: for him, the oracle is stupid, because it told him to do what is wrong, namely, kill his mother. The scene is both terrible and on the edge of humor: the matricide is approaching, but it is Electra forcing her less than heroic brother into the heroic role. When Orestes does kill his mother (he covers his eyes; and Electra's hand—she boasts—is also on the sword), there is every reason to think of him as being caught up in a rush of actions he cannot quite escape from, but has no wish to continue. What makes a young man kill his mother is a very real question here indeed. Irony, self-deception, lack of will—a full range of internal motivations is set in play.

From these three examples, I think we can draw one immediate conclusion. While tragedy is always interested in why people behave the way that they do, different plays can have a quite different interest in the internal, mental processes of its characters, and explore them in different ways. To my mind, it would be as misplaced to develop an intense psychological portrait of Aeschylus's Orestes, as it would be to ignore the doubts, bullying, self-deception, and unwilling heroism at play in the portrait of Euripides' Orestes. (For many readers, there is a general development of interest in psychology from Aeschylus to Euripides as the fifth century proceeds.) For an actor, the aim must be to find the right style of self-presentation. The characters of Greek tragedy are always on a public stage, and the exposure of internal life, those violent, tumultuous emotions, takes place always within such a frame, and with an eye on the generalized type rather than the fascination with individual quirks. Adjusting to this change of perspective, it seems to me, is a basic part of preparing a role for the tragic stage.

There is one further brief conclusion we can draw. The back story of Greek tragic characters always includes other versions of the myth. It is hard to understand Sophocles'

Electra or Euripides' *Electra* without Aeschylus's great masterpiece, the *Oresteia,* with which both younger men were obsessed. Aeschylus himself always wrote from within his engagement with Homer's epics. Behind every Orestes, there is a cast list of Orestes figures. A modern audience may not share this imaginative vista, and a modern actor may find it simply distracting. But whenever an Agamemnon or Achilles enters the tragic stage he drags clouds of Homeric glory with him. Where this bites on an actor's preparation, however, is in how little work a script needs to do to create an expectation of, say, heroic nobility, and the impact this has on a performance today. Just as when a modern actor plays Winston Churchill or John F. Kennedy, certain attributes of power need not be slowly developed, so Agamemnon has an inevitable strut to his stride from his back story. This needs to be accommodated to any performance.

]]] [[[

Acting in tragedy is hard work. Zoë Wanamaker said of Electra, "I didn't imagine that I was taking the part home with me, but when we finished *Electra* the first time, my back went out; I got the flu; I slept for five days non-stop. This part is a killer, but she's also a meteoric soul, a luminous heroine."[20] Fiona Shaw struck the same note: "I was physically wrecked from it—lame, thin, ill. You're psychically playing with illness, starvation, and burning up enormous intellectual energy. It didn't do me any good, that. It did my soul good, but I don't think it did my body any good."[21] The journey into a role in Greek tragedy makes particular demands. It exposes the actor by removing the props of modern theater. It requires immense technical skill to learn how to deal with the formal requirements of its style of writing, while at the same time expressing the most searing and dangerous emotions. To develop a character needs a changed perspective to appreciate the style of self-presentation. A failure in any one of these areas can derail a production irredeemably. At the same time, the director has to deal not only with the hugely demanding lead roles, but also with a company where many actors may have one brief scene (the messenger, say), and with a chorus which must spend a long time reacting to the action of others. Yet when the physical intensity of tragedy is combined with its extraordinary poetry to explore the fragility and power of the human self, there is no greater theater and no greater height for an actor to achieve.

Chapter Four
Tragedy and Politics: What's Hecuba to Him?

It is extremely hard to explain fully why Greek tragedy has enjoyed such an extraordinary revival in recent years. For the last few decades, there has been almost no year when there has not been a major production of an ancient Greek play in London, and New York, Paris, Berlin, San Francisco are not far behind. In the space of a few years in the 1990s there were four professional productions of Sophocles' *Electra* in London and also touring the whole British Isles. Euripides' *Ion*, which had received no professional performance in Britain in the twentieth century, was staged four times by professional companies in London between 1994 and 2004 (and was turned into an opera too).[1] What might seem like small-scale productions of obscure plays receive huge amounts of media attention: Euripides' *Children of Heracles*, a play barely produced since antiquity, put on at the Loeb Drama Center, the university theater at Harvard, by Peter Sellars' American Repertory Theatre, for a three-week run, received a five-page article in the *New York Review of Books*.² Why has Greek tragedy become such a hot property?

One part of any answer to this question must be that the political thrust of Greek tragedy seems particularly attractive to modern producers, directors, and actors. Tragedy's repeated concentration on the violence that emerges from the pursuit of justice, on the corruption of power in the pursuit of war, on the humiliations and misplaced confidence of the aftermath of military victory, on the battleground of gender within social order, seems to speak directly to the most pressing and dismaying of contemporary concerns. We have already seen how a string of modern productions explicitly cue contemporary politics in their staging, and we will see similar attempts to bridge the gap between the past and the present by contemporary translators in chapter 5. David Leveaux, director of Zoë Wanamaker in *Electra*, makes the point sharply: "*Electra* is not an obscure classic, a strange story of a distant time and place and people. It is, in every sense, our story."³

Drama has to strike such a chord in an audience. It cannot be just a preserved monument to its own classic status, like a salmon under aspic. But this does not mean that the politics of tragedy is a straightforward business, or that updating these plays comes without really tricky problems for a production. How should we think about tragedy and politics?

The Ancient Context

As in previous chapters, the ancient world provides a crucial framework for understanding the modern potential—and problems—of the political power of Greek tragedy.

Each of the Greek tragedies we possess was originally written for a single performance in a competition at the Great Dionysia, a festival of the god Dionysus, in Athens in the latter part of the fifth century.⁴ The three playwrights in the competition were selected by the state (the *polis*), and full financial support for the production was provided by an individual sponsor, again chosen to shoulder this considerable tax burden by the state. It was a principle that every citizen should attend the festival, and that no thought of loss of earnings or poverty should prevent participation. So a fund was set up (it is not clear exactly in which year) that paid the cost of the entrance ticket for any citizen who wanted to claim the subsidy. This subsidy was thought so important that it was against the law even to propose to change the law that set up the fund. So even when the state was desperately threatened by the financial pressures of war, the fund was sacrosanct. (How many modern companies dream of such support . . .) Going to the theater was a mass, civic occasion, fully supported by the state.

When you walked into the ancient theater, it was like walking into a map of the city.[5] There were special seats reserved for the five hundred members of Council, the executive body of government. There were special seats for the "war orphans," young men about to join the army (we will see why shortly). Each of the major wedges of seats was probably reserved for one of the ten tribes, that is, the sociopolitical divisions of the state. There was a separate wedge for foreigners and resident aliens. The front seats were reserved for priests and for foreign dignitaries. There were perhaps fourteen thousand people present—more citizens gathered together than at any other point in the calendar, except for the most cataclysmic battles. The theater seating displayed the organization of the state: political groups, age classes, outsiders. It was not only the plays which represented the city to itself.

Before the plays started, there were four rituals, each of which again shows the heavy involvement of the state in the occasion. The festival day was opened with a sacrifice and a libation of wine, as almost all major festivals were. But on the occasion of the Great Dionysia, the libation was poured by the ten generals, the most important political and military leaders of the state. The generals very rarely performed like this as a body—but they did every year at the Great Dionysia. It put the whole festival under the authority of the state.

The second ritual was a display of tribute monies from the allies of the Athenian empire. Members of the empire were forced to pay tribute, ostensibly to pay for the troops to protect the Greek world against the threat of invasion from Persia, but in reality to bolster the Athenian military forces and its power in the Mediterranean. (Attempts to leave the alliance were crushed with merciless and violent punishment.) The ambassadors of allied states were required to bring this tribute to Athens just before the festival of the Great Dionysia, and then they sat in the front row watching their silver processed around the theater. It was a ceremonial which declared the dominance and grandeur of Athens. It celebrated Athens as the leading power in the Mediterranean.

The third ritual was the announcement of the names of civic benefactors who had specially benefited the state during the year and had been presented with a crown. The Athenians themselves described this event as a way for the state to exhibit its thanks in order to encourage all citizens in their civic duty. One of the prime tenets of democratic ideology was that each man should act to benefit the collective of the polis. This ceremonial projects such a belief in ritual form. It staged the obligations of citizenship.

Finally, there was the presentation of the "war orphans." These were young men whose fathers had died fighting for the state (in the Athenian system of gender asymmetry, the death of your father made you an orphan). These youngsters were brought up at the expense of the state, and educated by the state. At the end of their maintained childhood, they were presented with a suit of armor, and in front of the collected citizens in the theater, they publicly took a moving oath. They promised to fight in the military force of the city and to be prepared to die for the city, as their fathers had before them.

Then they took their special seats in the theater. Since Athens was a warrior culture, where every man had to fight in the army or navy of the city, this was a moment when the full weight of civic, military ideology was powerfully performed in front of the citizens. It is another ceremonial which displayed to the city what it meant to be Athenian.

Each of these four rituals was designed to project and to promote the values of the democratic state and the proper ideology of participation in the state for the citizens gathered to observe them. Together these rituals framed the festival of the Great Dionysia as truly a civic event.[6]

That this is the occasion at which tragedy and comedy were both produced is quite flabbergasting to modern political sensibilities. Tragedy depicts a world in which all the values promoted in the ceremonials and the festival itself collapse. Tragedy portrays a city at war with itself, families and city in conflict, families in conflict with each other; a world in which security is constantly undermined by self-doubt. In tragedy, imperial victory leads to horrific costs; military ideals lead to vicious pain; contributing to the community becomes a crushing problem or foolish hope. At the same time, comedy makes fun of all that the city holds sacred, and turns everything into a carnival of misrule. The earnest self-control of the citizen is mocked, as the comic hero is led by his stomach and his penis into more and more farcical humiliations. Modern democracies contrast their lack of censorship with the official control of totalitarian regimes, but even contemporary Western society finds Greek tragedy a challenge to our sense of political order. How could a state-organized festival encourage such provocative and challenging performances? How could such a grand ceremonial event, lauding the state and its power, be the frame for images of social disorder and personal collapse?

Before trying to answer these fundamental questions, two preliminary conclusions from my description of the Great

Dionysia must be underlined. First, tragedy in ancient Athens was a political event in itself. It was not commentary on state policies, nor just a place where the arty classes saw art. It was a huge collection of citizens participating in the business of state ritual and engaging in the duties of democratic citizenship. Tragedy was a complex and troubling education into the values of citizenship. Second, the contrast with modern public culture, with its resolute fear and repression of serious debate, problematic issues, and challenging notions, is all too eloquent. It is the public, political seriousness of tragedy which so excited revolutionary thinkers such as Shelley, Wagner, and Brecht. That tragedy can be a challenging and moving political experience is not the fixation of modern directors: it is built into tragedy and the history of tragedy from the start.

]]] [[[

So how can we understand the role of tragic plays in city life? One strand of an answer compares tragedy and comedy. Fifth-century comedy is usually set in Athens, it has stage characters who are like their audience—Athenian, male, "ordinary"—and it stages familiar institutions—the law court, the Assembly, the theater itself—and even mocks powerful members of the audience by name. It is very much a theater of the here and now, for all that everything is passed through the lens of comic distortion and fantasy. Comedy shows Athens not as it is, but made other by the wand of comedy.

Tragedy, on the other hand, is enacted elsewhere. Nearly all our tragedies take place in cities other than Athens: *Medea* in Corinth, *Oedipus the King* in Thebes, and so forth. The exceptions are very few indeed: the *Oresteia* ends in Athens, but an Athens in the far mythic past. *Oedipus at Colonus* takes place in Attica, the territory of Athens, and at the beginning it is made clear that Athens can be seen someway in the distance. Tragedy is also set in the far past. It takes place at the time of the Trojan War or in the generations before. The only exception to this is Aeschylus's *Persians* (the oldest playwright is in many ways the most radically experimental). The *Persians* is set in the recent past of the failed Persian invasion of Greece, against which many of the audience including Aeschylus himself had fought. But this play is set in Persia, at the court of their enemies—as far from Athens as possible.

Nor are the characters of tragedy like the audience. Tragedy focuses on kings, heroes, monsters, women—all of which are conceived to be *other* to the male, enfranchised adults of the democratic citizen body. Tragedy, that is, unlike comedy, is set in other places, at other times, and involves other people. Tragedy is staged at the scene of the other.[7]

You might think that this gives a clear structure to the Great Dionysia as a whole, which explains the production of tragedy. The ceremonials and the festival laud the city as a city and celebrate its democratic principles, and then we are shown plays set elsewhere where society goes terribly wrong. Together, the good news of the ritual and the bad news of the tragedies produce a message for the citizens of what a good city is: Athens is a democratic haven; in Thebes they kill their fathers and sleep with their mothers. So let us celebrate Athens as the true home of civilization.

But there are two good reasons why this neat model won't work. The first is that the heroes of tragedy just are not simple negative figures, examples of transgression to be dismissed as a warning. Even Oedipus, the man who kills his father and sleeps with his mother, is said by the chorus of the play to be a paradigm for *all* mankind (as Freud later in his own way insisted). Oedipus is someone who wants to know where he comes from, who his parents are, and feels the need to be in control of the narrative of his own life. Who could say that Oedipus as a searcher after knowledge is not a figure for themselves? There are almost no characters in tragedy who correspond to the villain in a black hat. Part of what makes tragedy so enthralling is the complexity of the moral, intellectual, social positioning of its heroes and heroines.

This leads directly to the second reason. Tragedy may be set at the scene of the other, but it turns out to be about us. Hamlet, when he sees the Player weep, wonders "What's Hecuba to him?" Why should he care about a Trojan queen of ancient myth? Yet each performance of *Hamlet* sets out to make its audience cry at the story of a Danish prince of long ago. Tragedy raises questions about each of us, our sense of self and self-knowledge, yet to do so it takes a detour through the other. What look like stories about others, prove to go to the heart of the self. Indeed, it is *because* tragedy takes this strange detour that it can be so powerful. It gets past the censor, the checkpoints that prevent an audience's engagement with the staged action.

Let me give an example to make this last point clear. It is a story told by Fiona Shaw and Deborah Warner about taking the production of Sophocles' *Electra* to Derry in Northern Ireland.[8] The week before the production had been a bad one in the Troubles, and several people had been shot dead. It should be noted that both John Lynch (Orestes) and Fiona Shaw (Electra) are Irish and speak with an Irish accent. But even so, the response of the audience took everyone in the company by complete surprise. There was no applause at the end; almost no one left; and the audience demanded to discuss what the play meant to them, politically, ethically. This happened each night of the run. *Electra*, as we have seen already, is a play that harshly exposes the human costs of a desire for violent revenge. It shows up the psychological damage of violence even or especially when pursued in the name of justice. Had a modern play been produced that talked about the troubles, the audience may have had a wide range of responses. But partisan politics, disagreement with one particular narrative in so complex a history, self-consciousness, even a simple wish to say "no" to any aspect of the play, can all put a barrier between the audience and the action. Because the play was set in a far distant place and far distant time, none of these resistances came into operation. The drama took the audience to a place it could not have reached without the detour of tragedy's otherness.

Ancient tragedy in Athens gives us the remarkable spectacle of a society prepared to allow its most cherished political and social values to be questioned on the largest public stage the city could offer. But it does so *not* by staging contemporary political action or characters, but by turning elsewhere: tragedy uses the drama of otherness to question the self. This seems to me to go the very heart of the politics of tragedy.

Contemporary Politics: Finding the Right Distance

By contrast with the performance of *Electra* in Derry, the production of *Trojan Women* at the National Theatre in London in 1995 tried too hard to make a political point, and failed.[9] The chorus in this production were refugees and war victims from around the world: their collective identity was the product not of any social group per se, but rather of the production's political stance. The relation between the chorus and Hecuba, Cassandra, and Andromache was consequently watered down, and Euripides' sense of the fragility of burgeoning sympathies and consolation was lost. But, most annoyingly, the Greeks appeared in American uniforms and with (poor) American accents. This staging waved a sloganizing political banner: "Americans are responsible for imperialist violence and the suffering it causes." As a blunt political point, it failed to engage the spectators at any real emotional or intellectual level. The largely English audience saw their prejudices either about Americans or about left-wing directors confirmed. In the *Trojan Women*, it is the gradual recognition that the increasingly horrible suffering of the victors is being enforced by *us*, the Greeks, which makes the play so challenging. The Trojan War played a major symbolic role in the Greek imagination: it was the first great victory of the West over the East, and stood as a model for the defeat of the Persians (Athens' greatest moment) and for all subsequent wars. The play builds from an initial sympathy to more complex feelings of anger and grief, which are complex precisely because the play speaks about our own behavior, ideals, and blindnesses. By making the Greeks into Americans, the National Theatre production let the audience off the hook. And they remained disengaged.

The contrast between the reaction of these audiences in Derry and in London highlights an important set of questions for any production: how are the links between the past and the present constructed? How is the significance of these old plays for today to be drawn out? How is the contemporary relevance of an ancient play to be brought to light?

The route taken by Warner in her *Electra*, and by many others, of course, is to aim for what is often called a "timeless" production. (The "timeless" beauty of Greek tragedy was one of things that the nineteenth century loved about it, especially in German culture.)[10] This allows the audience to make its own connections, and to reach toward its own emotional engagement with the play. So Zoë Wanamaker reflecting on the set of David Leveaux's *Electra*, commented, "It could be Sarajevo, or Northern Ireland, anywhere, really. What David is saying—what we as a company are saying—is: what happens to the children of war? . . . How do they grow up? How do they go through life as normal human beings after what they have been through?"[11] Although Wanamaker says the play could be set anywhere and sees the questions it raises as general ones, she nonetheless immediately reaches for modern parallels—Sarajevo, Northern Ireland. This is how the production hopes the audience will react, and certainly the critics enacted and encouraged such a response.

In the play, Wanamaker wore a greatcoat and boots (which in the 1990s became something of a standard costume in Greek tragedy on the London stage). It neatly showed up Electra's strange relation to her gender: as an unmarried woman who is fierce and violent, Electra is scarred by her assumed masculinity in the Greek imagination.[12] But the image of the greatcoat works precisely because of its historical associations. It draws on contemporary images of contemporary war zones. The rubble around the palace door in this production was both modern furniture in pieces and bits of Greek-style masonry. With a rather pleasing irony, this points out all too clearly how "timeless" is a theatrical convention, designed to bridge the ancient and the modern. As the chorus, with postmodern enthusiasm, announced in Aidan Carl Mathews's *Antigone*, one of three *Antigones* produced in Ireland in 1984, "The drama is set in Ireland in the 1980s BC, soon after Sparta had entered the war on the German side."[13] "Timeless" is always just such an artful mix of costumes, sets, and props with specific connotations, a jumbled historicity which aims to prevent a close connection with any particular period and thus to proclaim its generality.

The advantage of such a setting is clear (apart from any financial and practical considerations: greatcoats are cheap, rubble readily available). It focuses attention on the acting and the action itself, it avoids the immediate distractions of a contemporary political scenario, and, above all, it gives space for the particular tragic dynamic of engaging the self of the audience through the suffering of the other. The "timeless," however, can itself become a fashion victim. Because the greatcoat was *the* costume of tragedy through the nineties, it runs the risk now of becoming a cliché: a sign of the classic status of a play, and of the theatricality of the event. What works as "timeless" changes over time.

When so many of the plays chosen for modern production from the Greek repertoire concern either the buildup or the aftermath of war, it is not surprising that a more specific battle zone has often formed the basis of a staging and of a political agenda. Perhaps the most important factor in the political impact of these plays is how the idea of "distance" is manipulated by a production.

To see the importance of "distance," it is fascinating to compare two of Katie Mitchell's productions: her *Oresteia* at the National Theatre in London in 1999, with a script by the poet Ted Hughes, and her *Iphigeneia at Aulis* also at the National five years later in 2004. The *Oresteia* production at one level wanted to have its cake and eat it: "The design and visual world of Katie Mitchell's production attempted to create a timeless area, while making reference to the twentieth century, and in particular to the post WWII era," wrote the production team.[14] It is hard both to be timeless and to refer to the modern age. In fact, the references were far from casual: "We researched images from throughout the century, particularly those depicting hardship and conflict. Photographs of the Balkan conflict and the excavation of mass graves provided powerful and disturbing evidence which fed directly into the Old Man's report."[15] This strategy was aimed precisely at bridging the gap between past and present: "Contemporary references, designed to reduce barriers, meant that audiences, distanced by the historical nature of the play, would not be able to say 'this has nothing to do with me.'" The belief here is clear: it is through contemporary references that an audience can be engaged in ancient tragedy. As for so many poorly thought-out government educational policies, for the education department of the National Theatre, it would seem, history is alienating, and only the contemporary is relevant.

The contemporary "references" were full elements of the staging. Clytemnestra had a large NATO briefing map covered with black arrows for her tracing of the return of Agamemnon; Apollo appeared as a Red Cross doctor; the chorus of the *Agamemnon*, seated in wheelchairs like a line of Beckett heroes, took out typewriters and tape recorders in their long first ode, which retells the buildup to the expedition to Troy, acting as old journalists, commenting on the action; Orestes and Pylades as the Phokian strangers were dressed like Balkan Mafiosi (complete with droopy mustaches); the Furies appeared as if in a torture chamber. For almost all reviewers, and most of the audience, one suspects, this was not so much a few "contemporary references" as a setting in the Kosovo of Milosevic.

For one reviewer (in the *Daily Telegraph*, the most conservative of the English broadsheets), the production, by virtue of these gestures toward today, was deeply patronizing: "She is constantly underlining just how modern, just how relevant Aeschylus's great masterpiece is. . . . The audience is never allowed to draw its own conclusions." Although Hughes's translation was "deliberately timeless," the production proved to be a "glib anti-war morality play."[16] Others were more sanguine, and called it a true "production for the millennium" (many plays vied for this title in 1999, at least in the prose of the critics). The *Guardian*, the most left-wing of the broadsheets, in its turn worried that the real political problem was with the *Oresteia*: "It posits a belief in the advance of history and the progress of civilization that, at the end of a tormented century, we passionately wish were true, but cannot convincingly share." For this critic, the modern references reminded him of a contemporary world so bleak that even Aeschylus's tragic vision looked excessively optimistic.[17]

There are, no doubt, many reasons why these reviewers express themselves as they do. And we can be sure that Aeschylus's masterpiece resulted in conflicting political understandings at its first performance, too. But it is clear that the critics are responding with differing degrees of discomfort to the lack of distance in the production. The closer the play comes to being "set in contemporary Bosnia," or "about the contemporary situation in the Balkans," the *less* gripping, the *less* convincing it seemed. Where the production team thought contemporary references were necessary to break down the barriers of historical distance, the reviewers found that it was precisely the modern notes that were blocking them from the big questions of "what is good?" "who is God?" The audience's discomfort was a product of what they saw as the play's inadequate construction of distance.

Iphigeneia in Aulis in 2004, the second Katie Mitchell production, also had a military setting. The scene was a mess hall or barrack hut near the military camp of the Greek expedition. It was set roughly at the time of the Second World War. The women who visited the camp to see the military heroes had dresses in late thirties, early forties style, with handbags and high heels. The music complemented this setting, as did the old-fashioned microphones and other equipment onstage. The play exposes the desperately mealymouthed and bitterly self-serving rhetoric of the men who make war, and the women's increasingly horrified and traumatized response to it. The production had a sardonic clarity in this exposure, which became extremely moving, especially when the effects of the ideological war machine were seen in the figure of Iphigeneia, a little girl in her undershirt and knickers, ready to die for the state and what her father said was right.

There will always be critics who will complain about such a historically located production that it is "not Euripides"— and in this case, some critics did so, volubly and aggressively. But the majority found this a finely evocative dramatic occasion, and even critics who disliked the production found the clarity with which the political rhetoric was exposed to be strikingly articulate. There was no doubt that this play had a political agenda aimed at contemporary society. Yet the distance the drama imposed by setting its action away from the present (but in a scene that was familiar enough) allowed the audience to engage in that agenda without feeling patronized. The play was dramatically revealing, rather than preaching. The contrast between the two productions reveals just how fine the line can be between necessary distance and engaging relevance.

One alternative to the mishmash of "contemporary reference" or the distance of historical setting, is a full-on modernization. Peter Sellars, the one-time wunderkind of American theater, has produced Greek tragedy regularly ("every five years when things get dangerous," as he himself put it).[18] His production of the *Persians*, translated by Robert Auletta, was performed first in 1993 at the Salzburg Festival in Austria (bizarrely enough), and then at the Edinburgh Festival in Scotland before opening in Los Angeles.[19] This aggressive and loud version of Aeschylus's play took the logic of distance to the opposite extreme. Auletta simply played the Greeks as Americans, and the Persians as Iraqis, and interspersed the play with modern music and contemporary military information, complete with references to Rambo, B-52s and cluster bombs. Darius toured a children's hospital without electricity, where mothers rocked their dying babies in their arms, before delivering a grim warning to the Americans sitting "comfortably in their capitols/smiling, playing golf, appearing on television/ and speaking of their great achievements." It was a blunt, in your face, experiment. (His chorus spat out, "I curse the name of America," and bitterly called the Americans "terrorists" who are "experts at applying sanctions—to garrotte a country, cut off its vital life of trade, suffocate and humiliate its people" in pursuit of oil.) When audience members in Los Angeles walked out—a hundred a night, every performance, at different times, as each spectator found a personal sticking point—it was, they said, because the play gave a voice to the Iraqis, enemies of the United States, and this voice expressed pain, as well as contempt and hatred for America. "The Gulf War was one of the most censored wars in the history of journalism," wrote Sellars, and he wanted to get past that censorship, and he did so with a long scream.

I suspect that the walkouts would have pleased Sellars no end (as well as being good publicity). A good shock out of complacency is perhaps the beginning of the education that he hopes theater as a social force can provide. Here was no question of "contemporary references" or historical distance: the play was directly made as a play about today, while still trying to hold on to the cachet of the classics. It made a political point, it used the ancient tragedy as a medium to do so, and in its demand for empathy for a defeated enemy caught something of the true force of Aeschylus's play. The *Persians*, significantly, is the only one of our existing tragedies to tell the story of historical events close to the audience's own time and experience. This makes it peculiarly ripe for Sellars' treatment, and a unique challenge to the logic of tragedy's distancing devices.

One of the very earliest plays we know anything about was a tragedy called *The Sack of Miletus* by Phrynichus, who was writing in the generation before Aeschylus.[20] The play was about the Athenians' failure to support their allies in Miletus, who were viciously crushed by the Persian military forces. The play so upset the Athenians that it was banned—consequently, we have almost no idea what it was like—and the author was fined a huge sum. It upset them, we are told, specifically because it recalled their own personal sufferings. If tragedy gets too close to its audience, it will be resisted. It becomes a different sort of political theater. Tragedy needs a detour though the other to make its emotional and political points. Negotiating this necessary distance is a requirement of any production, if it is to find a way of letting its audience fully engage with the politics of tragedy. *Finding the right distance* is a fundamental process in producing Greek tragedy.

Political Preaching: Antigone for Today

War, with its passionate sense of "us and them," puts a special pressure on the requirements and difficulties of distance. But this is only one area of tragic politics. Tragedy is also repeatedly concerned with the relationship between the individual and the state, and the conflicting obligations and loyalties of citizenship. No play of the ancient world has been produced as often in modern times as Sophocles' *Antigone*. It is a play which inevitably brings these political questions of citizenship and power to the fore, and it is precisely for this reason that it has been so often produced. But *Antigone* also raises the question of the degree to which tragedy preaches a political message. Does Sophocles' play have a clear political agenda, and, if so, how does it speak to a contemporary audience?

The stories are legion. Jean Anouilh wrote his version of *Antigone* during the Second World War in Paris, and it was produced under Nazi occupation. The Nazi censors found Creon's arguments convincing and were happy to give permission for its performance—while the French audience reveled in Antigone's resistance. So the story goes: in fact, the politics were far more complicated. Not only was Antigone also seen as a dangerously suicidal self-interested martyr, but in a production shortly after the war the French audience even cheered Creon's words about social order.[21] A performance of *Antigone* was put on in No-Man's Land in the collapsing former Yugoslavia. Soldiers were the extras. The question of how the state and the individual interrelate is nowhere more pressing than in civil war—but we have no reactions recorded from the soldiers participating in this drama. Perhaps most famously of all, a production of *Antigone* was staged at some point in the 1960s in a South African prison with Nelson Mandela as Creon. *Antigone* was, Mandela tells us, one of his favorite books in his long imprisonment, and subsequent history has made this all too poignant.[22]

Athol Fugard's *The Island* was first performed in South Africa in 1973 under the apartheid regime, and since across the world. It is a response to the stirring story of one member of his own fledgling multiracial theater group who was sent to

Robben Island Prison on a trumped-up political charge, and managed to put on a two-handed production of the conflict of Antigone and Creon—in a way that was not censored by the authorities but still spoke thrillingly of political freedom to his fellow prisoners.[23] *The Island* is not an adaptation of *Antigone* but a play about putting on *Antigone* in prison. Yet it reveals vividly a central dynamic of Sophocles' play, and why modern performances of ancient tragedy have something special to contribute to the political imagination.

The question of distance and the political impact of tragedy is raised explicitly in the play, focused on two political prisoners, John and Winston. John has been trying to teach Winston the outline of the plot of "The Trial of Antigone," which he wants them to perform. It has taken Winston a long time to pick up the basics. But Winston has now just refused to play Antigone, once he has realized it means dressing as a girl. He is ready to pull out altogether:

WINSTON. Go to hell, man. Only last night you tell me that this Antigone is a bloody . . . what you call it . . . legend! A Greek one at that. Bloody thing never even happened. Not even history! Look, brother, I got no time for bullshit. Fuck legends. Me?, I live my life here! I know why I am here, and it's history, not legends. I had my chat with a magistrate in Cradock and now I am here. Your Antigone is child's play, man.

Winston's anger, his need to hold on to his current suffering, his own history, rejects the old story as "bullshit," something that did not happen, and therefore of no relevance to him, in the here and now. What's Antigone to him? But John immediately counters by seeing such talk as giving in to the intimidation from their guard, Hodoshe

JOHN. Winston! That's Hodoshe's talk.

WINSTON. You can go to hell with that one too.

JOHN. Hodoshe's talk, Winston! That's what he says all
the time. What he wants us to say all our lives.
Our convictions, our ideals . . . that's what he calls
them . . . child's play. Everything we fucking do is
"child's play" . . . when we ran that whole day in
the sun and pushed those wheelbarrows, when we
cry, when we shit . . . child's play! Look, brother . . .
I've had enough. No one is going to stop me doing
Antigone.

For John, to reject the political debate of Antigone as child's
play is to become complicit with the desire of the prison
guard, Hodoshe, to denigrate, humiliate, and crush the political aspirations of the prisoners. "Doing Antigone" is an
act of political resistance. It can be performed because it is a
classic play, a legend; but not only will they promote through
their "Trial of Antigone" a political message of opposition to
the repressive state, but also the very performance itself is an
empowering act of resistance. *Antigone* is seen as a means of
taking convictions and ideals seriously—and without convictions and ideals, what is politics? What is the point of the here
and now of history?

At one level, the final act of *The Island*, which is the performance of "The Trial of Antigone," makes a simple and
powerful political point about the need for resistance to the
brutalizing power of the state, and as such validates Antigone
over and against the harsh Creon. That would seem to be its
political message. But there has been a far more subtle development through the play between the two prisoners, Winston
and John. For the first half of the play, John is pushing, cajol-
ing, and nagging Winston into his role as Antigone. But as
they change roles, and Winston takes on the role of Creon, a

change also takes place in the relationship between the two prisoners. John has been told that his sentence has been commuted, and Winston torments him with his imaginings of the outside world, making the slow passing of time unbearable. That is, as they swap roles in "The Trial of Antigone," so the power dynamic of their own relationship shifts. Playing Creon puts Winston in a position of dominance; the promise of freedom undercuts John's drive for resistance (fig. 12). The relationship between the two men plays out the conflict of *Antigone* at a different level, and frames "The Trial of Antigone"

12 John (John Kani) and Winston (Winston Ntshona) as Creon and Antigone in Athol Fugard's *The Island.*

with a complex portrayal of the attractions and corruptions of power, and the inevitability of domination in human social relations.

This sense of the complexity of conflict, where there is right on both sides, where positions shift, where audience sympathies falter and veer, is fundamental to Sophocles' play—and to tragedy in general. In *Antigone,* both central characters, Antigone and Creon, start from positions which are fully validated in cultural terms. In Athenian democratic culture, it is right, as Creon says, to act on behalf of the city. A man should commit himself to the state, and the traitor is a monster who should be expelled and destroyed. So, too, it is also a normal, privileged position to fight for your own family.[24] The desirability of the continuity of the family is one value that does not change through hundreds of years of Greek history. Yet this play is also about what happens to such good values when they are not in harmony (as the standard ideology of the state and family would have it), but when they come into tension with one another. Then these standard moral positions become distorted into extremes. Creon's commitment to the state as a principle of duty and obligation becomes a tyrannical wish to rule by his own word as head of state, and to maintain the rule of law at whatever cost. Antigone's commitment to family values leads her to destroy herself, to ruin any chance of the family continuing, and, for the sake of a gesture toward the dead family, to bring violence and misery to the living family. Antigone's sister, Ismene, who tried to maintain a middle road, is useless at persuading either her sister or her uncle. She achieves nothing; and dramatizes all too painfully the inevitable failure of middle-of-the-road reasonableness in the face of extremism—which is one reason why this play speaks so strongly to modern society.[25]

This dynamic, whereby two powerful morally justified positions become hardened into self-destructive extremisms— leaving the audience no place to go, no character simply to associate themselves with—has proven very hard for modern theater to follow. *The Riot Act*, with script by the poet Tom Paulin, and directed by Stephen Rea, is an excellent case in point. This version of the *Antigone* was produced in Derry, Northern Ireland, in 1984, when the Troubles, the violent conflict between Protestants, Catholics, and the British government, were especially brutal and intense, and it has been widely read, produced, and discussed since.[26]

The setting of the play is not given in the script, though it is clearly a small, conflicted community, where religious division and a strong family loyalty are pervasive. The language of the script is based on short, harsh colloquial sentences, with plenty of Northern Irish expressions (and expressiveness). This all encourages the connection with the here and now without an explicit parallelism. This suggestiveness can be handled with real subtlety. Ismene, for example, in the opening scene, says, "I heard, though, / the Argives pulled out last night." The Greek says, "The Argive army has gone . . ." But the phrase "pulled out" precisely recalls the language of the TV reporting and the bulletins of the warring sides in the Troubles. That makes even the otherwise normal expression "The Argives" sound like a paramilitary organization or a brigade of the English military forces in Belfast. Paulin has a fine ear for working the Greek into a taut, contemporary language.

But Paulin is nothing if not politically passionate himself, and he has a very clear agenda in this play. When Ismene in this first scene refuses to join Antigone's desperate plan to bury her traitor brother, she does not reject the plan because of the weakness of their shared gender or because of the power of the law (both reasons are given in Sophocles), but because of what will happen to them if they are caught in such an act. They will be punished by an angry mob, and Paulin is surely thinking here of the street conflict of Northern Ireland:

ISMENE. Can you imagine, but,
        what way we'll die—
        some scraggy, smelly crowd,
        us dragged before them—
        oh, they'll spit,
        they'll sleg us then,
        shout all the dirt
        till the first stones go whap!
[Smacks hands near Antigone's face]
        and go on thumping us.
        Don't tell me it's not right—
        that's what is!
        Would you have me cry
        for some great change
        out there in nature?
[Points at audience]

Ismene's speech starkly imagines mob rule (and conjures up the baying crowds and violent hostility of sectarian hatred). What is more, she turns the accusation directly at the audience. While her phrase "out there in nature" makes her thought a generalization, the instruction to point at the Northern Ireland citizens in the audience makes it plain where the blame for her fear is being laid.

The writing of the part of Creon shows this strategy of linguistic modernization and political pointing in the most developed form. His first great speech marks him out as a politician, a politician in the sense of a mistrusted, public figure, whose self-interest and love of power distorts his already fierce ideological position. He begins with a set of platitudes, designed to evoke the blandest political speech—the sort that always most masks power:

It therefore gives me great pleasure to report that public confidence and order are now fully restored, and, if

I may, I would further like to take this opportunity of thanking each and every one of you for your steadfastness and your most exceptional loyalty.

Paulin again pinpoints the awful linguistics of civil war. Talking of the restoration of public confidence and public order is always a sign of the desperate hope of the powers-that-be that conflict in the community will have ended. Creon's speech is indeed grimly prophetic of the political rhetoric of more recent times:

> For my own part, I have always heard that one of the soundest maxims of good government is: *always listen to the best advice.*

It is a blunt, but still painful irony, that Creon can depict himself as the "government that listens." Where Creon in Sophocles' play begins with political maxims that the vast majority of the audience would recognize as the norms of civic life, Paulin's Creon is undermined from the start. He is already marked by his shallow rhetoric, his glad-handing, power-broking, self-interested politicking. This is all the more evident in the argument with Haemon. For Creon in Sophocles, the punishment of Antigone is a question of the necessity of the rule of law, and, like all good Greek patriarchs, he sees family discipline as an analogy to order in the state. In Paulin's version, Creon's case has a far harsher, blacker undertow:

> CREON. Obey your father
> that's the only nature.
> If we've no law,
> nor right discipline,
> there's no trust either.
> I've seen children

chuck both parents over—
blood on the walls
and the whole street laughing!
I've watched good men wrecked
by some hard-nosed bitch . . .

In the modern West, the simple demand for a son to obey a father marks the father as an unthinking bully, and the brief generalizations of Creon move from his image of a father laughed at by the street, toward a restatement of his own authority, delivered in personal terms:

So let me tell you,
I'll not back down.
I made that law—
the law is clear;
she broke it,
on her head be it.
She betrayed the state
and she betrayed me.

"I made that law": Creon's personal investment in the law is emphatic, and the motivations for his firmness are excruciatingly placed under scrutiny.

Creon's final collapse—the death of Antigone, the suicide of his son, the suicide of his wife—are seen in Paulin's play as the result of Creon's own stance, the flaws of which are revealed by Antigone's opposition. But from the start Creon is depicted as a horrific man, smug at first in his public appearance, pushed into hypocrisy, bullying, and violence, as soon as he is crossed. Paulin is attacking the political leaders in the Troubles (and their imitators and enforcers on the street). The portrait of Creon is designed to show how the moral stance of the leaders, veined as it is with more personal investments, leads to social divisiveness. "I wanted Creon to be a kind of puritan gangster, a megalomaniac," said Paulin, "who spoke alternatively in an English public school voice and a deeply menacing Ulster growl."[27] It is a play that charts the tragic consequences of Creon's destructive politics. The final words of the play rub in the message:

> CHORUS. When men get proud, they hurl hard words, then
>   Suffer for it.
>   Let them grow old and take no harm yet: they'll still get
>   punished.
>   It teaches them. It teaches us.

The didactic thrust is brought home. Not just the "them" but the "us" need to learn to lose the pride, the hardness, if suffering is to stop in the "us" and "them" conflict of civil war.

The Riot Act is an interesting play, acutely attuned to its time, and powerfully written. But in one respect it offers a quite different dynamic from Sophocles' play. Creon cannot be allowed to have a case. For Paulin, Creon's position leads to suffering because it is wrong, not, as in Sophocles' play, because it is right (but not right enough). It makes (as one might expect from Paulin) for a far less subtle political posture. Paulin indeed explicitly says that he was writing the play as an attack on the political writer Conor Cruise O'Brien, who had pointed out in discussing Northern Ireland how complicit the Antigones were in the continuing violence. Paulin dismisses Conor Cruise O'Brien's wish for compromise and his support for Ismene in stark terms. For Paulin, to side with Ismene is to side with Creon. "Life is about tragic choices," he declared; "Know which side you're on. Know what principles you espouse."[28] Paulin is for Antigone. Full stop. And his *Antigone* reflects this fully.

Greek tragedy is a remarkable genre of public literature because it questions, challenges, destabilizes the public discourse of the state. It asks hard questions, but very rarely indeed provides anything that looks like an answer. Most of the people in Greek tragedy who think they have the answer—confident like Oedipus, committed like Antigone, strong like Ajax, intent like Medea—end up suffering terribly for their certainty. Tragedy again and again manipulates an audience's sympathy, so that typically even those who appear first as maltreated victims—like Hecuba, like Medea—end up committing acts so horrific that any sympathy is sullied. Tragedy does not like to have a character with whom an audience simply associates and through whose eyes the play is viewed. This all makes tragedy's politics uniquely provocative. It takes cherished beliefs, splits them apart under pressure—but puts nothing back in their place. It lets you see the cracks in the edifice of social life.

Many modern directors insist on offering large didactic messages through ancient tragedy ("war is brutalizing," "Americans are imperialists," "power is evil"). These more often than not merely confirm the prejudices of the audience, and would challenge only a hypothetical spectator who thinks in equal and opposite slogans ("war is ennobling," "Americans civilize the planet," "power is love"). Ancient tragedy has the rare ability to probe under the skin of its audience, to expose the fragility of certainty, to nag away at the posturing and secret desires of all politics. This dynamic is lost when directors give in to the desire to tell the audience some certainties of their own.

Tragedy is a lure for political didacticism: in my view, the temptation should be devoutly resisted. It should be resisted not because tragedy cannot speak powerfully to contemporary politics: far from it. The history of theater shows just how often the performance of Greek tragedy has had an extraordinary impact on the political imagination. But tragedy is at its most powerful politically when it draws an audience to recognize the tensions and fissures within its own views, its own ideals; and when it goes beyond the local and the parochial.

That is tragedy's special power, which is always concealed when directors preach.

Gender Politics

Greek tragedy, like Shakespeare's plays, was originally acted only by men. It was also written by men, and acted before an audience that was probably of men only. What is more, the texts of tragedy have often been seen as founding texts in the history of patriarchy. The *Oresteia* in particular has played a long running part in feminist thought. As Tony Harrison wrote, when considering why his *Oresteia* was played by an all male cast, "Though it is a fact that men played all the parts of *The Oresteia* in 458 B.C., that in itself is not of course sufficient justification for our wish to have an all male company. The victory of father-right over mother-right is the social pendulum of the trilogy. To have women play in our production would have seemed as if we in the twentieth century were smugly assuming that the sex war is over and that the oppressiveness of the patriarchal code existed only in past times. The maleness of the piece is like a vacuum-sealed container keeping this ancient issue fresh." Harrison asks that we see the maleness of the cast of the *Oresteia* as a demand for continued political thinking about gender in modern society, a refusal to believe that an answer to the "ancient issue" has (smugly) been found. This is a paradigmatic example of how Greek tragedy's fascination with gender politics has been instrumental in its modern flourishing.

This is not just a product of the late twentieth-century women's movement. In the nineteenth century, versions of *Medea* (written by men) were already being staged as satirical commentary on the Marriage Act, which prevented women from holding property of their own and restricted the rights of wives drastically.[29] But one of the most striking developments in the last quarter of the twentieth century (and still today) is the burgeoning number of adaptations of ancient plays made with an explicit agenda from within the politics of gender. Tony Harrison's *Oresteia* continues his political point about casting with the language of his translation. The *Oresteia* sets man against woman, male against female. The trial of Orestes in the *Eumenides* turns on the question of who the true parent is, mother or father. The language of the play is full of explicit indications of a conflict between the genders, from the Watchman's opening remarks that a "man-plotting woman's heart" has set him to watch, through to the final decision of the court. But Harrison emphatically underlined this focus in his version. Zeus is "Zeus the high he-god," Artemis is a "she-god," and when Agamemnon takes Iphigeneia for a sacrifice, "so a father can take his own she-child take her / and kill her his she-child his own flesh and blood." At every step, the audience was reminded that gender is a marked term in this trilogy. Interestingly, when Apollo declared that the father is the only true parent, and that the mother is nothing but a nurse to the seed that is implanted, there was no laughter at what might be expected to sound like a ridiculous claim to a modern audience. Even when Apollo stated that "the womb of the woman's a convenient transit"—a line that might seem comical—the logic of the play was too clear, and the patriarchal claim drew a sharp intake of breath.

Greek tragedy writes some great parts for women (including older women): Medea, Electra, Phaedra, Hecuba. In every case, these women are set in opposition to men, and the conflict at some level turns on gender. In every case, the female acts initially to preserve the household against a threat of destruction perpetrated by a man. In every case, by virtue of this opposition a woman is led not just into violent conflict with men but also into self-destructive acts of a horrific nature. What is more, male figures (and some female) are happy to offer what to a modern audience must sound like rank misogynist rhetoric. For Greek traditional thinking, from

Pandora onward a woman is a "beautiful evil," a "discordant harmony," as Euripides' female chorus of the *Hippolytus* puts it. Tragedy is not a good place to be a woman.[30]

Because these stories have both such prestige in theatrical history and such a hold over the imagination, Greek tragedy has been subject to all sorts of adaptation from the perspective of a modern gender politics. John Fisher's *Medea: The Musical* was produced in Los Angeles in 1996. It had begun in student theater (as plenty of its comedy showed) but had lengthy runs also in San Francisco and won several awards. The plot is not easy to describe. A company is intending to put on *Medea* with a gay Jason. Paul, the actor who plays Jason, *is* gay, as are all the male members of the cast and crew. The female cast members are all straight. When Paul/Jason falls in love with Elsa/Medea, life and art mix, and gender stereotypes also start to unravel. Paul is put under pressure by the gay community not to pursue Elsa. Elsa and Paul conspire to make a feminist *Medea*. Elsa cannot see why any intelligent woman would leave home for a man "who offers her nothing but a little adventure and the occasional screw" (a view which might be thought to ignore literary history as well as showing little empirical awareness). They want a new Medea who will make sense to women too. Nor do they want a Medea who kills her children: when Paul insists that "killing your children is a feminist act. It's the ultimate act of self-empowerment. It is like burning your bra," Elsa retorts, "No. It's a woman hurting herself to hurt the man she loves because he no longer loves her. It's a man's idea of a feminist act." The couple break up before the opening night, however, and Paul appears as Jason in drag—a red kimono, high heels, and a big blonde wig. In the musical, Phaedra and Hippolytus are visiting Medea's family home. Jason makes a play for the pretty Hippolytus. Elsa—not to be outdone—declares her passion for Phaedra. Jason and Medea jointly sacrifice their children (played by adult men), and the play ends in a suitably comic scene of riotous festivity.

Medea: The Musical is funny, camp, parodic, and thoroughly modern. But it also shows well the strategies of radical adaptation of tragedy. First, *Medea: The Musical* depends on the audience having some sense of ancient myth. The more knowledge of the ancient stories an audience has, the more resonance the playful rewriting of plot has and the more comic pleasure it allows. But all that is required for the play to work is a general sense of *Medea* (the woman who kills her children) and an awareness that sexual attitudes in society are formed through a long history of culture, in which the classics play a major role. Second, the point of rewriting the old stories is not just comic mayhem. The musical which Paul and Elsa are to star in is meant to "create a space for the homosexual on stage," with multidimensional gay characters. The play itself is highly self-conscious of sexual stereotypes, and revels in playing with them, and teasing the audience with slippery sexual identities. (As the author John Fisher inimitably sums up the plot of Euripides' play: Medea "fucks up Jason's whole patriarchal structure too, and then she flies away in her dragon-drawn chariot laughing maniacally. It's like *yeah*.") There is a serious point underlying the comedy—which the performance itself, with its high camp and drag, helped make. Rewriting the myths of the past is a way of challenging the place of old myths in the contemporary cultural imagination. "Challenging the myths" is an easier aim to declare than to achieve, however. It is noticeable that the play was extremely happy to celebrate the ideal of the Greek male body (a value-laden stereotype from the ancient past). And parody also inevitably pays homage to its models. *Medea: The Musical* undertakes this project of challenging some of the traditional stereotypes of sexuality through comedy and parody. Many other plays have taken this task very seriously indeed.

There have been a great number of such rewritings, particularly by small, experimental companies. Inevitably, most of these adaptations have not entered the repertoire, even when they have had a local success, and most are recorded only in theater archives. But, collectively, they are a sign that a modern performance of tragedy has to be acutely sensitive of the politics of gender. A modern production of *Medea* will necessarily find Medea viewed through modern political concerns. This will affect also the misogynist speeches of a Jason or a Hippolytus (or Creon or Eteocles or . . .). What is crucial to remember is that such speeches are never just ridiculous bluster or cold hatred. The antifemale rhetoric in Greek tragedy comes out of a social background that did repress and control women to a very significant degree (just as modern sexism has deep social roots); Hippolytus and Jason take to an extreme attitudes prevalent in ancient Athens, and although their extremism will provoke an audience in different ways, it is also clear that it is part of their journey toward destruction and despair. As with *Antigone*, where standard commitments to state and to family become distorting and self-destructive extremisms, so too masculinity's self-assertion becomes a violent and self-destructive spectacle. Tragedy kicks at the struts and props of maleness, and nothing is more at risk in tragedy's arena than the secure boundaries of masculine self-definition.

The scripts of Greek tragedy inevitably reflect their genesis in a society that is quite alien to us—but also frighteningly familiar. Patriarchy is the oldest game in town, and Greek culture is an authoritative image for the West's idea of itself and its history. (Greece is the fatherland from which patriarchy comes.) But tragedy, for all its misogynist rhetoric, also asks profound questions about the security of the male in his masculinity. The task of the modern director is to see beyond the insults or stereotypes which tragic characters throw around, in order to reveal the more subtle undermining of the certainties of gender.

Conclusion: Tragedy and Politics Today

Tragedy's politics is a detour through the other to expose the cracks in our edifice of self-knowledge and self-assertion. Modern productions need to observe these dynamics of distance, if they want to tap into tragedy's special power. Tragedy, whatever some of its characters do or say onstage, is not a preachy genre. It asks questions, uncovers divisions, exposes tensions, in the politics of gender as well as in the spectacles of power. Directors have most impact when they avoid behaving like one of the characters of tragedy, and do not insist on telling everyone what is certainly true. The omens are not good for those who make such pronouncements.

Tragedy still has the power to influence the political imagination. Bill Clinton, ever the master rhetorician, when he visited Northern Ireland to help in the peace process, famously recited lines from a modern version of a Greek tragedy, Seamus Heaney's *The Cure at Troy*:

> History says, *Don't hope*
> *On this side of the grave.*
> But then, once in a lifetime
> The longed-for tidal wave
> Of justice can rise up,
> And hope and history rhyme.
>
> So hope for a great sea-change
> On the far side of revenge.
> Believe that a further shore
> Is reachable from here.
> Believe in miracles
> And cures and healing wells.

These lines were delivered in Derry at a moment of great hope—and had their desired rhetorical effect. Perhaps it helped that Mary Robinson, the Irish prime minister had also quoted them earlier in a political speech, and so too had the Irish minister of foreign affairs (which says something of how far these lines have entered modern consciousness).[31] But it is typical of the deep-seated irony of the politics of tragedy that at the very moment of proclaimed optimism, we cannot help but hear a grim undertow. "History" and "Hope"—as the poet knows all too well—can never quite rhyme, except by an act of will and deafness. The ability of tragedy to uncover and display the fissures and tensions in political idealism, political power, and even political hope, is rare in the public discourse of the modern world, and for that reason all the more needed today.

Chapter Five

Translations: Finding a Script

Vladimir Nabokov translated copiously, and hated it, with a passion that only a man who wrote in his second language could feel. He made a terrible translation of Pushkin's *Eugene Onegin*, and wrote a couple of stanzas of doggerel about how much the task induced self-loathing. He ends:

This is my task—a poet's patience
And scholiastic passion blent:
Dove-droppings on your monument.

For Nabokov, to translate is to defile the poet's monument with repeated small insults.[1]

In the best of all possible worlds, Greek tragedy would be performed in ancient Greek. As with Puccini in Italian, Shakespeare in English, Racine in French, there is a rhythm and music to the Greek language which is wholly lost in the work of the translators, traitors all. The verse form of the dialogue and speeches—described by Aristotle as the closest to human speech—has a sinuous flexibility, the choral odes a rhythmic drive, and the whole script a musical beauty which is transfixing. If there is a chance to hear or see a play in ancient Greek, it should be taken.

But . . . almost all modern productions will need to find a script, and the most common question I am asked is "what translation do you recommend?" This is a hard enough question to answer when it is asked by a literature student who wants just to read Greek drama. It is even harder once all the other demands of a theatrical performance are brought to bear. Many of the best productions I have been discussing have developed translations for particular performers, particular resources, or particular political or cultural circumstances: however enticing the script may seem, it is hard to restage *Gospel at Colonus* without a gospel choir. Similarly, great performances have been made out of what appear to be rather dull versions—it is still something of a surprise that Fiona Shaw's intense passion as Electra came from Kenneth McLeish's characteristically restrained script; by the same token, what seem like great translations can be butchered by a performance. What's more, translations, too, like all theatrical forms, are prey to fashion and can slide out of date quickly. I want first to discuss here some of the different routes taken by contemporary theater to finding a script, and, most importantly, what some of the implications and results of such choices can be.

There are many translations on the market which are designed primarily for school or university classrooms. I have focused here, however, on texts that have been designed and used for productions, largely on the professional stage. This is because the difference between textbooks and scripts is stark. The first word of the *Bacchae* is *hêkô*, literally, "I am come." It is a striking beginning, announcing the presence and threat of Dionysus, in human guise. Standard classroom translations offer: "I, son of Zeus, have come to Theban soil," "I, Dionysus, son of Zeus, have come to the land of Thebes," "I am Dionysus, the son of Zeus," "I am the son of Zeus, Dionysus,"

"I am Dionysus," "I have arrived"—none of which is incorrect as a version of the Greek.[2] The extremely experienced team of Frederick Raphael and Kenneth McLeish, however, have "You see the son of God. I have returned."[3] This, for me, is in a different league of writing for the theater, a truly gripping beginning to the play. This is the sort of translation I will discuss.

The Grandeur of Aeschylus

Each of the great Greek playwrights brings different difficulties of translation. I will begin with Aeschylus, and will stick with translations into English (although there is plenty of relevant material in German, Italian, and French, of course). Aeschylus writes extremely dense, highly imagistic poetry, with long, rolling sentences, where the grammar is often tortured, and the vocabulary a daunting combination of magniloquence, shimmering metaphors, and bold juxtapositions. There are dozens of translations of the *Oresteia*, with immense varieties of style. To begin our discussion, let us look at some of the lines that Cassandra delivers in the great scene of the *Agamemnon*, where she delivers her prophecies to the unbelieving chorus, before processing off to her death. I have chosen to look at these lines because they are not quite as difficult as some of the lyric verses, and yet capture a good deal of the difficulty of Aeschylean writing. Here is a basic translation of the lines (*Agamemnon* 1178–93), an academic version by Hugh Lloyd-Jones, former professor of Greek at Oxford, which aims to get in all the Greek words with accuracy and some precision:

> Now shall my oracle be no longer one that looks forth
> from a veil, like a newly wedded bride,
> but as a bright, clear wind it shall rush
> toward the sunrise, so that like a wave

there shall surge toward the light a woe far greater
than this; no more in riddles shall I instruct you.
You bear me witness, running beside me as I scent out
the track of the ills accomplished long ago!
For this house is never left by a choir
that sings in unison, yet with no pleasant sound; for not
    pleasant are its words.
Yes, and it has drunk—so that it grows all the bolder—
of human blood, and stays in the house, a band of revelers
not easily sent away, composed of the Erinyes bred within
    the family.
And the song they sing as they beset the rooms
is one of destruction that began it all; and each in turn they
    spit
on a brother's marriage-bed that brought harm to its violator.[4]

This is not a translation anyone would recommend for the stage, nor is it great literature, but it provides a benchmark against which to look at versions which have been staged. Cassandra promises a clear prophecy, but her language remains intricately allusive and metaphorical. The opening six-line sentence mixes up the images of wind and rain and sun, and the final image of the chorus of Furies, blood-drunk and singing in the house, is tied to the story of Thyestes' adulterous crime—unnamed in the last grim lines. (Thyestes slept with Atreus's wife: Atreus killed Thyestes' children in return and fed them to their father. These are the sins of the fathers of Agamemnon and Aegisthus.) Cassandra is keen to persuade the chorus that she knows how the horrors of the family of Atreus started, and she tries to control her wild mantic language into a more restrained expression. Even so, the dense vocabulary and complex syntax swirl with the passionate inspiration of her vision.

By way of contrast, here are some lines from a script that was written specifically for production, and was very widely seen. This is Raphael and McLeish's *The Serpent Son*, the text used for a very starry BBC production in 1979 (with Diana Rigg as Clytemnestra, and Helen Mirren as Cassandra, as well as Claire Bloom, Dame Flora Robson, Sian Phillips, and Anton Lesser). It takes a very different approach to Cassandra's prophetic voice:

> No more riddles now. I'll tell it plain.
> Now my prophecy is no shy bride
> Peeping out from her veil; it is a wind
> That hurls the morning waves
> Full in the sun's bright face.
> I'll speak no more riddles. There's worse to come.
> You are my witnesses, hunting as I hunt,
> Hot on the scent of ancient wickedness.
> Above this house there hangs a raucous choir,
> Furies clamouring with malice,
> Plump with human blood. They dance
> Sarabands of death in the palace halls.
> They are a crouching horror, spitting hate:
> "What was Thyestes' crime?
> Incest, incest: he slept with his brother's wife,
> His brother Atreus' wife."[5]

This translation takes Cassandra at her word when she says that there will be no more riddles. Her language is rigorously removed of ambiguity and allusiveness. Where Aeschylus does not indicate who the "choir" is that sings above the house for fully five lines, the Furies are named here as soon as possible. The crime of Thyestes is explained in a question and answer format (as if responding to an audience worry about names and back-plot). The long sentences of Aeschylus are all removed to short phrases, and the rich swirl of confusing images is neatened up. The speech remains touched by Cassandra's lyricism: the speech is more imagistic than most in the script, and allows itself small moments of a more incantatory zeal ("incest, incest . . . his brother's wife, his brother . . ."). This is a script for television, notoriously resistant to long sentences, complexity of verbal imagery, dense metaphors; but it demonstrates perfectly one coherent response to translating Greek tragedy: reduce, control, streamline. Zoë Wanamaker captures an actor's pleasure in such a style of translation, talking of Frank McGuinness's version of Sophocles' *Electra*: "Frank's adaptation was pared down to the very fishbone; it's clean as a whistle; it's English I can understand—sometimes slightly crass, sometimes slightly raw, sometimes slightly strange to the ear, but it is accessible to me."[6] The dense poetry of Aeschylus is filleted by McLeish and Raphael precisely in the name of accessibility. The tension between the familiar theatrical aim of such instant comprehension and the *Oresteia*'s strange choral majesty and architectural, nonrealistic action is particularly violent. But Ken McLeish, often writing with Freddy Raphael, has proven one of the most popular of translators for precisely this skill in offering actable, clear, ungrand, unpoetic scripts.[7]

Such streamlining followed the production values of *Serpent Son*, which took a largely naturalistic style of acting, in line with the television's need for close-ups. (For a production like Mnouchkine's *Atrides*, a translation like this would be quite out of place.) The simple syntax, blunt vocabulary, controlled expressiveness, will find an acting style to match. The problems with such a translation are most evident with scenes like the great mourning song of the *Libation Bearers*, sung by the chorus, Orestes, and Electra around the tomb of Agamemnon, where unlyrical bluntness sits uncomfortably with a long, emotional ritual song. Or with the appearance of the gods, when a certain grandeur seems necessary; or with the long choral odes, where Aeschylus's most intense poetry sustains the length and complexity of the narratives. Aeschylus, of all the tragedians, resists the drive toward simple clarity and a naturalistic aesthetic, and, in my view, a translation needs to respect this.

It is instructive to compare the Raphael and McLeish translation with Tony Harrison's version for the National Theatre. Harrison's poetic voice is instantly recognizable. Here are the same lines:

> Off with the brideveil then. Look into truth's pupils
> The truthgust. It's rising. Blowing fresh headwinds
> sweeping sea-ripples into dawn's molten cauldron,
> then building a woe-wave as big as a mountain.
> Riddles are over. Keep close on my track now
> as I scent out the spoor of ancient transgression.
> Listen. The rooftops. Monotonous humming
> that drones on forever and means only terror.
> The blood-bolstered fiend-swarm holds its debauches,
> cacophonous squatters that can't be evicted,
> chant over and over the crime where it started
> cursing a bedbond a bloodkin defiled
> trampling all over the flowing bed-linen.[8]

Harrison's verse has an insistent rhythm, reinforced by his aggressive alliteration. His jagged portmanteau terms create a mountainous language out of simple words. The syntax can be tautly direct ("It's rising," "Listen," "Riddles are over"), and yet the sentences can roll on and on, culminating in a five-line description of the Furies. As in Aeschylus, the nature of the crime is addressed only allusively, but in powerful and clear language. This is poetry designed for a more incantatory style (even with the touches of contemporary Yorkshire: "squatters who can't be evicted"). This was for a formal, stylized delivery, in a production with an abstract design and grand-scale stage. It recognizes Aeschylus's lyric intensity, allows his swirls of language, and is unafraid of the sheer boldness of the *Oresteia*'s poetry.

Where Raphael and McLeish strip down the language to a
bare simplicity, designed for a naturalistic, plot-driven, family
drama, Harrison's poetry leads toward ritual, incantation, a
stylized aesthetic. What, then, of Ted Hughes, whose production (directed by Katie Mitchell in 1999) followed Harrison's
at the National Theatre in London? Here, again, are Cassandra's lines:

> You want to know?
> I'll rip away these bridal veils
> Where prophecy peeped and murmured.
> I'll let it go like a sea-squall
> That heaps the ocean and piles towers
> Of thunder into the sunrise—
> I'll bring out a crime
> More terrible than my own murdered body
> Into the glare of the sun.
> No more mystery. I will show you
> How far back
> The track of blood and bloody guilt
> Began, that now sets me
> And Agamemnon and Clytemnestra
> Face to face today.
> This house is full of demons,
> The loathsome retinue
> Of the royal blood.
> Under these painted ceilings they flutter and jabber.
> They huddle on every stair
> They laugh and rustle and whisper
> Inside the walls.
> They shift things, in darkness
> They squabble and scream in the cellars.
> And they sing madness
> Into the royal ears. Madness.
> Till the royal brother defiles the bed of his brother.[9]

Hughes's version is by far the longest we have looked at, nearly twice as many lines as the Greek original. Most strikingly, he has provided a clear and direct narrative, with precise syntax, no rolling, long sentences, no confusion of conflicting images. He wants the audience to understand absolutely that Cassandra is taking the chorus back to the origin of the family problem, and is giving us a picture of a family curse. He expands this account with his picture of the Furies, who have become somewhat more like English ghosts than the Greek chorus who gorge on human blood. It is hard to see how this Cassandra could be misunderstood or not believed (whereas Aeschylus's verse, like Harrison's, is darkly multivalent). Hughes, however, has provided a much blanker canvas than either Harrison or Raphael and McLeish. In the first performance of Hughes's text, Lilo Baur, who played Cassandra, stole the show with her mad cries through the veil, desperate tones, and final brutal and shocking display of her abused body. This *Oresteia*, as we have seen, was broadly criticized for its naïve antiwar rhetoric, but also reached toward a stylized production (with its chorus of typewriting journalists in their wheelchairs). Hughes's translation is rhythmic, speakable, and with a strong sense of narrative drive. This allows for a range of approaches, of which Katie Mitchell's Royal Shakespeare Company's production is only the first. But it provided a vehicle for a passionate, moving, and highly dramatic performance, which is precisely what is wanted. In some ways, Hughes's verse gives more scope for the director's and actor's creativity than either Raphael and McLeish's terseness or Harrison's bold incantations.

These first three translations were each used for major and widely seen productions. They obviously provide very different scripts from the same passage of Greek—and each is fully consistent with the three very different styles of production that they received in their first performances. There are two simple points that follow. First, the style of translation has evident and immediate consequences for the potential of the staging and the form of the production. The choice of translation will help determine the nature of the dramatic event. It makes as little sense to try for a naturalistic performance style with Harrison's word-mountains as to try for a grand, stylized production with Raphael's and McLeish's clipped control. Second, all translators pay lip service at least to "fidelity": "My main objective in producing this translation of the *Oresteia* is to produce a work that is accessible, performable and dramatic while retaining a fidelity to the Greek."[10] But Greek tragedy is often difficult, dense, and highly poetic—a language modern theater usually resists. There is always a difficult calculation to be made between losing the power of the ancient form and communicating with a modern audience. The problem is familiar from Hollywood's remakes of Shakespeare or Jane Austen in modern language and dress (which can be inspired, as with *Clueless*'s redrafting of *Emma*, but are all too often crass). If clarity or accessibility is made the dominant aim of the script it will have severe implications for the choral odes in particular, which in turn will affect the whole shape of the play. In short, the script and the style of performance are mutually implicative choices. So the first answer to "what is the best translation?" must always be "for what type of performance?"

The Politics of Translation

In the last chapter we looked at how contemporary politics enters Greek drama today, and the importance of tragedy's politics for the modern popularity of ancient tragedy. Translators direct such politics. Brendan Kennelly is a fascinating case in point. He has translated three classical texts so far, *Antigone*, *Medea*, and *Trojan Women*.[11] His version of *Antigone* was the third version produced in Ireland in Orwell's year, 1984 (I have already mentioned the postmodern show of Aidan Carl

Mathews, and the one-sided politics of Tom Paulin's production). For Kennelly, whose translation is in many ways the straightest and simplest of the three Irish *Antigone*s, Antigone is a "feminist statement of independence." This sense inflects his translation at crucial points. As Antigone processes toward her entombment and death, she responds to the chorus's patronizing and all-too-late gestures of sympathy:

> Men are leading me to death.
> Men made the law that said I'm guilty.
> Men will place me
> In a black hole among the rocks.
> Men will deny me light.
> Yet all I did was for a man
> Whom other men called evil.
> Because I could not kill my love,
> My love kills me.
> In this place, killers of love go free.

Antigone laments her coming fate in Sophocles' play, and the funeral language she uses marks her out specifically as a virgin who dies before marriage. So too in each of the great arguments—between Antigone and Ismene, between Antigone and Creon, between Creon and Haemon—gender becomes a briefly mentioned but intensely fought battleground. But the strong emphasis on masculinity as the cause of the action in this ode is Kennelly's. The hammer blow of the monosyllable "men" at the beginning of each line bashes home the point. This is even more striking in the following lines, with which Antigone again upbraids the chorus of men:

> You are used to flattering men.
> But I am a woman
> And must go my way alone.
> You know all about men,

You know all about power,
You know all about money.
But you know nothing of women.
What man
Knows anything of woman?
If he did
He would change from being a man
As men recognize a man.

Antigone's loneliness, which Sophocles briefly draws out, is expanded here to a full-scale political position. Men's failure to understand women—and concomitant commitment to the unholy coupling of money and power—makes men what they are, and only a redefinition of masculinity in the eyes of men can lead elsewhere. For Kennelly's Antigone, the political argument between Creon and Antigone becomes an all-out gender war. This is in striking contrast with Paulin's *Riot Act*, where gender is repressed as an issue throughout, in his pursuit of his own political agenda. Ismene, it will be recalled, does not even use the argument of the weakness of their shared femininity as an excuse for not acting: instead she reasonably fears the violence of the mob. Two translations, in the same city and in the same year, lead into quite different political agendas. The impact of the politics of the translation will be felt throughout any production.

Euripides' *Medea* does not touch on the politics of the state in any way like the *Antigone*, but it brings gender into the limelight even more strongly: Tony Harrison's ill-fated version (an opera libretto of the whole story of Medea rather than of Euripides' tragedy) is actually titled *Medea: SexWar*, and its only professional production was interspersed with readings from the manifesto of *SCUM*, the Society for Cutting Up Men.[12] Brendan Kennelly's version of *Medea* is nearly 50 percent longer than Euripides', and the material which is added takes the play in a specific, political direction. In her famous first speech, Medea wins over the chorus (to the fascination of the audience) by her speech about a woman's lot in life. It is a speech that has often been taken up in a feminist cause, often without regard for the fact that it is a speech designed to suborn fellow women by its manipulative appeal for solidarity ("we women . . ."), and is delivered by a barbarian witch who will go on to murder her own children. In Euripides' Greek, Medea begins her exposition of the awful state of women with (in my own translation) (232–34):

> First, with an excess of money, we have to buy
> a husband, and take a master for our bodies.
> This second is a still more painful evil than the first.

The dowry is sarcastically described as "buying a husband" (as if a husband were a slave or chattel, and as if the wife paid the dowry anyway), but the paradox is that what is bought is not a slave but a "master," a master over the body of the wife, which is even "more painful" than the humiliation of the marriage. Kennelly expands these lines in characteristic style:

> First, all dressed in white, for the most part,
> we are the playthings of men's bodies,
> the sensual toys of tyrants.
> Men, the horny despots of our bodies,
> sucking, fucking, chewing, farting into our skin,
> sitting on our faces, fingering our arses,
> exploring our cunts, widening our thighs,
> drawing the milk that gave the bastards life.

Kennelly explains that the keynote of his image of Medea is rage, "a devastating woman in a cell of rage."[13] And the character is certainly angry. The image of "master for our bodies" from Euripides explodes into a violent denunciation of sex as humiliation and abuse. Kennelly has said that part of the inspiration for his translation came from his time in a psychiatric hospital recovering from alcoholism, where he spent hours listening to women's "savage, pitiless and precise . . . rage against men." So "the Medea I tried to imagine," he explains, "was a modern woman, also suffering a terrible pain—the pain of consciousness of betrayal by a yuppified Jason, a plausible, ambitious, articulate opportunist." She "plans to educate Jason in the consciousness of horror." The play opens the door on this horror, and leaves both Medea and Jason painfully sentenced to a life in it.

This image of Medea resulted in a range of very strong reactions when the play was produced in Dublin in 1988. And that is where the question of this powerful translation lies. The dynamic of this speech is wonderfully precise and complex in Euripides' play. It is essential for the unfolding of the play that Medea here should evoke the sympathy of the audience, as well as its fascination through her manipulative rhetoric, along with an underlying recognition of danger. When she says, "I am not like you, your friends and family and home are here; but I have no mother or brother . . . ," we do remember that she fled from her family home, and murdered her brother to escape. "I have no brother" is a breathtaking rhetorical claim, funny and awful in the same breath. There are audiences for whom Medea's words in Kennelly's version will strike precisely such a chord. But there are also audiences who will react against her violence of expression, and be alienated from her character. The choice of a translation like Kennelly's will depend on evaluating the benefits and costs of its very strengths: here is a powerful piece of writing that may split, provoke, and challenge an audience, but here is a piece of writing that for the same reasons may alienate an audience from Medea at the moment when she is most seeking after sympathy.

To set Kennelly's translation in the starkest light, here is Alistair Elliot's translation for Jonathan Kent's production

starring Diana Rigg. Elliot sets out, he tells us, for an "uncluttered, transparent, close translation" where "Euripides'
dialogue has been honed down to a film director's rapidity."
He sticks to the three lines of Euripides' original Greek:

> First we must throw our money to the wind
> To buy a husband; and, what's worse, we have to
> Accept him as the master of our body.[14]

This seems to me to fulfill rather well the aim of "uncluttered, transparent, close translation," although perhaps the
paradox of buying a master is underemphasized slightly. Raphael and McLeish take this paring down to an even further
degree:

> We scratch and save, a dowry to buy a man—
> And then he lords it over us; we're his.[15]

"Scratch and save" adds a note of bourgeois thrift quite
missing in Euripides (a woman, after all, does not provide
her own dowry); and the lack of any mention of the body in
this translation takes away a sexualized precision which is always important in this play. It is as a woman "wronged in the
matter of sex" that Jason categorizes her anger. For Raphael
and McLeish there is no politics of the body in this conflict
between husband and wife—while for Kennelly it dominates
the rage of Medea. The translation that a production chooses
will bring to bear a different gender politics, and will produce
a play with a quite different focus and emphasis.

Politics is one area where translations date most rapidly.
Tom Paulin was confused and upset to see a revival of his
play *The Riot Act* in Oxford in the late 1990s. The production
had bleached out what he regarded as the specific politics of
his script and turned the play into a more generalized, timeless setting. It set Paulin to wondering in his characteristic

manner how Thatcher's children, the students who grew up with Margaret Thatcher's legacy of individualism and lack of social duty, could not appreciate or live up to the political ideals of the generation of the 1960s. (*Après moi . . .*) But for the audience fifteen years after the first production, Paulin's script had lost its polemical and contemporary edge.[16] Aidan Carl Mathews, author of another of the Dublin Antigones of 1984, had the text of the Criminal Justice Bill solemnly sounded from a tape recorder as a playback of Creon's argument with Antigone, and kept it running during the interval. This is unlikely to have the same bite twenty years or more on. Tragedy can transcend the parochial, and find a world of meaning in the grains of local political rows. But the more localized the translation, the harder it is to go beyond its self-imposed limitations.

Gender politics is one of the most sensitive areas of this problem of dating—not because patriarchy is fading, or at least not because patriarchy has ceased to be a real issue. Rather, there are shifts in the politics of gender that are harder to trace than the passing of the Criminal Justice Bill. I suspect that there are more women who would be insulted by the use of the word "cunt" in a theater (especially in a piece written by a man) in 2005 than in 1989, and more so in America than in Europe. If this is true, it becomes a live issue for how the audience's sympathy will function with Kennelly's portrayal of Medea. Translations bring their own politics to the table, and a production will be led by such an agenda. Choosing a translation will not determine the politics of a production, but it will strongly influence it in one direction. To inhabit a script is to inhabit its politics, and this makes the choice of a translation crucial to the political impact of the play. In chapter 4 I argued that distance was crucial to the political effect of tragedy. The more a translation wears its politics on its sleeve, the less this necessary distance can be calibrated. Ancient tragedy only very rarely made direct, local political comment, and yet was doing politics at the most emotive level. Translators can learn from this.

The Chorus and Translation

The advice that the actor and director Stephen Rea gave to Tom Paulin as he embarked on his translation of *Antigone*, was "Go easy on the chorus, they can be a bit of a bore."[17] In chapter 2, I discussed how the chorus is one of the founding problems for any modern production of Greek tragedy. We saw there how the change of expressiveness in the choral odes was one of the trickiest transitions to manage in the staging of the chorus. It is equally difficult for a translation. The choral odes are the hardest part of any tragedy to translate. The poetry is the most dense, the syntax most convoluted, the imagery most intricate, the narrative most allusive. Most translators seek to make the odes more easily comprehensible, for perfectly obvious dramatic reasons. The danger of such simplification is that the odes will become banal generalizations, cliché-led reflections on life, or trivial, brief poems without passion, surprise, or the raging power of Greek lyric language. Such oversimplifications produce clarity for an audience but problems for a production. Can the chorus discover the different form of expressiveness their role demands? Can the odes have enough emotional and intellectual drive to stop the audience finding them "a bit of a bore"? The choral ode needs to combine a level of writing that takes them beyond the language and style of the scenes, with an openness to performance. Finding a translation that matches up to this stiff criterion is part of what makes the chorus such a problem for modern production.

Many translations do not even try. The choral odes are written in approximately the same style and meter as the scenes. The most dull embodiments of the chorus—the standing-still and intoning-wisdom choruses—all too often are drawn toward or encouraged by these more prosaic translations. But the lyric voice of the chorus also flourishes in amazing exuberance. Let's look at a choral ode from Sophocles' *Antigone*. After Creon and Haemon have argued so vehemently and Haemon has fled the stage, the chorus sing a short ode on desire, *eros*. It acts as an explanation of the previous scene, suggesting that Haemon is motivated by sexual desire for Antigone as much as by his more abstract arguments about power, and it also looks forward to the next scene of Antigone's march to the tomb, where her sexuality as a virgin facing death is integral to the intricacy of her portrait. The ode is not long, but it is dense in its imagery and narrative.

Here, first of all, is the version by Timberlake Wertenbaker, one of the most prolific and successful of translators of Greek tragedy for the stage. This was used in *The Thebans*, a production of *Oedipus the King*, *Oedipus at Colonus*, and *Antigone*, staged by the Royal Shakespeare Company in Stratford and London at the beginning of the 1990s, directed by Adrian Noble.[18]

Desire
Never bested in battle
Certainly not deterred by wealth
Desire
keeps vigil on a girl's soft cheek
lingers over the sea
trickles down lairs in the wild.

No armor in immortality
Eros
even less human
ephemerality
where you are, there is madness

with you, the just turns unjust; the
mind is wrenched aside. Destruction.

With you, enmity ejects kinship. You
stirred up this battle between this
youth, this man.

Triumph in the wistful eyes of this
most beddable bride.
Desire
curls around the oldest laws.
What does it matter what is or is not
allowed
when
Aphrodite wins all?

Wertenbaker's scenes have long, rolling lines, which flow with strong direction and forcefulness, particularly in the rhetorical arguments. They require good breath control and technique, and demand extended attention—and are well fitted to the acting style of the Royal Shakespeare Company, trained as they are in Shakespearean iambics. Here, in the choral ode, the verse becomes chopped, with single-word lines, and heavy enjambment for significant effect. As the chorus declares "the mind is wrenched apart," so the verse wrenches the word "the" at the end of one line from the word "mind" at the beginning of the next, performing the act of wrenching apart. The syntax is simple, as is the vocabulary, but the lyric poetry reaches intense levels by juxtaposition and the strangeness of the imagery: desire "curls around the oldest laws," a phrase to curl around the tongue as it is said, but whose sensuousness does not conceal the striking originality of the expression (which captures brilliantly the tension between their evocation of desire and the arguments about the law in the previous scenes). This sensuousness is particularly marked at the end of the first stanza where desire "keeps vigil on a girl's soft cheek, / lingers over the sea, / trickles down lairs in the wild." The repeated liquid sounds and images flow softly through the ode.

The syntax is hardest in the second stanza. "No armor in immortality" alludes to the inability of even the gods to resist eros. "Even less human" adds how humans cannot expect to be stronger than the gods. Interjected between these two traditional ideas are two single words, each a line. "Eros," the power that overwhelms even the gods; "ephemerality," the fragility of life which grounds human desire, and distinguishes men from gods. The final line, "where you are, there is madness," sums up also the mad splitting of voice in the stanza. The third stanza makes explicit the relation between the ode and the scene that has just passed: "you / stirred up this battle between this / youth, this man." The "battle between" is enacted in the verse again with the split between "you" and the verb, and between "this" and "youth"—a hesitation as the chorus open the possibility of other descriptions for Haemon (son? fiancé? brave resister? madman?). The ode thus climbs to its resigned or despairing conclusion about the invincible power of Aphrodite, goddess of desire.

The poetic intensity of the ode takes the chorus into a new realm of expressiveness. It offers a range of real opportunities for director and performers alike. These lines could be spoken in unison by a chorus, split between different members of a chorus, or even delivered by a single voice. It could be sung, spoken, or delivered in "singspiel." It could be danced, enacted, or a scene of stillness. What matters most here is the change of register, the quality of the writing, and the potential such poetry provides for different styles of production. This seems to me as good a modern version of a Greek choral ode for theatrical performance as there can be.

Compare Timberlake Wertenbaker's version of the ode with Brendan Kennelly's.

Love, you are the object of our lives;
Love, you are the truest crime;

Love, you prove the obscenity of money;
Love, you are a waste of time.

Love, you live in the heart of a girl;
Love, you are the spittle in an old man's lips;
Love, you are a suburban nightmare,
The soiled lace-curtains from which a heart escapes.

Love, you help a child grow up,
Love, you fill the eyes of a young bride;
Whatever they say of you, O Love,
You're always dying, yet never completely dead.

Love, love, love. . . . We are being invited into the world of
the popular lyric. The repeated address to "love" (rather than
desire), along with the simple, repeated structure ("you are
. . . you are"), may hope to look back toward William Blake's
Songs of Innocence and Experience, but drags the pop song with
it, or, worse, the "love is . . ." mug or some such similar grotesque cuteness of modern romantic fantasy. The lines veer
between the relentlessly banal ("love, you live in the heart
of a girl," "love, you help a child grow up"), the striving of
the angst-laden adolescent poet ("Love, you are a suburban
nightmare," "you are the obscenity of money"), and search
for paradox—the biggest cliché of all modern ideas of love
("Love, you are the truest crime"). The ode does act as a
hinge, although unlike Sophocles or Wertenbaker, it does not
draw out the point of its connection with the argument of
Haemon and Creon. Most obviously, it looks forward to Antigone's cry to the chorus in the next scene, "Because I would
not kill my love, / My love kills me."

This ode offers quite different problems of performance.
It does offer a changed register of expressiveness from the
scenes, but how is the ode to escape from the banality of its

writing? Perhaps the banality is the point. Perhaps, that is, the chorus reflect on love at this high point of tension in the drama, and can only reach for the banalities of popular culture, and this stands in ironic tension with the searing emotions either side of the ode. The chorus (as in Sophocles' *Antigone*) are throughout the drama ineffectual men, counselors cowed by the power of Creon and unwilling to express their own moral qualms till it is too late. Perhaps this ode, in line with such a characterization, shows their intellectual and emotional insufficiency. There are some high-risk opportunities here for the chorus to sing this lyric in accordance with such a characterization (in the style of a pop song), or to play up its banality. This would have huge implications for the style of the whole production, of course (*Antigone: The Musical*?). Perhaps the banality has to speak for itself: the standard types of remark on love ironically left hanging before the scenes of suicide and despair. The lines may read like a parody of a chorus's portentousness, but the performance should not be allowed to slip into parody—or portentousness—here. I have done my best to make sense of the translation. But I also feel it is fighting a losing battle. It seems to me that this ode provides considerable difficulties for any production. It sums up perfectly the problem I outlined in the first section of this chapter: when the dense poetry of lyric is sacrificed to clarity, you can be left with banality.

McLeish's popular translation of 1979 shows a different response to the apparent simplicity of Sophocles' short ode. Here is his version:

> Love cannot be conquered in battle
> Or bought or sold for cash.
> He is everywhere: encamped
> On a girl's soft cheeks,
> Riding on the barren sea,
> Peopling the wilderness.

When he shoots arrows of desire,
No god, or man can escape
His madness.

Love twists even a just man's mind
And turns it to evil and shame.
He stirred this present strife,
Son against father.
His arrows glitter in the glance
Of a fair bride's eyes;
He sits enthroned in power.
When his goddess, Aphrodite, plays,
She wins with ease.[19]

It would be harder to have a more "uncluttered, transparent, close" translation than this. Nor does it limit the production's options in style of performance. Yet, although it avoids the clichés and unhappy portentousness of Kennelly's version, it is hard not to feel that this lacks an emotive lyric voice. The rhythm is repetitive and plodding. The language is simple to the point of flatness ("he is everywhere"; "bought or sold for cash"; "love twists even a just man's mind"). The images are careful and unsurprising ("riding on the barren sea / peopling the wilderness"). Above all, it is hard to hear the seductive pleasure and unhinging threat of sexual desire echoing in this ode. Perhaps as a lyric for musical performance it could be carried into a higher region (the libretti of the most moving arias are often trivial when written down as mere words), but as an ode for speaking this seems to demonstrate the threat of the search for the "uncluttered, transparent, close" translation, namely, that in paring down the language and imagery of the ode, what is left is a bare and unmoving narrative.

Seamus Heaney is the latest in the long line of Irish translators of *Antigone*. His version was produced in 2004 in Dublin, again, which has hosted a profusion of modern performances of Greek tragedy.[20] His text has some terse, fast, and very speakable verse, especially in the opening scenes. (The play opens with "Ismene, quick, come here! / What's to become of us? / Why are we always the ones?") The guard speaks in prose to begin with, though finds himself in poetry as he describes the second miraculous burial of Polyneices and the capture of Antigone. Creon speaks in longer, more orotund verses. The language throughout is spare, direct, rhythmic, and easy on the ear. The choral odes are translated in full, and in the recognizable style of Heaney the poet. Here is the ode to Eros:

> Love that can't be withstood,
> Love that scatters fortunes,
> Love like the green fern shading
> The cheek of a sleeping girl.
> Love like spume off a wave
> Or turf-smoke in the air,
> Love you wield your power
> Over mortal and immortal
> And you put them mad.
>
> Love leads the good astray,
> Plays havoc in heart and home;
> You, love, here and now
> In this tormented house
> Are letting madness loose.
> The unabashed gaze of a bride
> Breeds desire and danger.
> Eternal, sexual, smiling,
> The goddess Aphrodite
> Is irresistible.
> Love mounts to the throne with law.

Heaney handles the repetitive invocation of love without any hint of the trivial pop song. His images are rooted in a specific rural Irish tradition ("like a green fern," "like spume of a wave or turf-smoke in the air"): the vivid simplicity of such images is powerfully evocative, especially after the general and blander "Love that can't be withstood, / Love that scatters fortunes." A sexual language floats through the second stanza in particular, not just in the explicit imagery of the "unabashed gaze" or the "sexual" goddess, but also in words like "breed," "mount." The combination of delicate, erotic imagery ("like a green fern shading / the cheek of a sleeping girl") with the more violent ("scatters fortunes," "plays havoc") embodies the combination of "desire and danger" which the poem articulates.

Heaney's poetry offers a simple but largely effective lyric. It could easily be set to music or performed in other vocal styles, collectively or individually. It takes the chorus to a new level of expressiveness, especially through the repeated invocation of love, and the juxtaposition of different levels of imagery, something the text elsewhere avoids. It has a greater sense of eroticism and threat than McLeish's simplicity, and less verbal intensity than Wertenbaker. It seems to me that this is also a text that invites performance. It is open to the imagination of a director.

The opening of Sophocles' ode inspired also the greatest Irish poet of the twentieth century. W. B. Yeats wrote an intense little lyric, "From 'The Antigone,'" which begins

> Overcome—O bitter sweetness,
> Inhabitant of the soft cheek of a girl—
> The rich man and his affairs,
> The fat flocks and the fields' fatness,
> Mariners, rough harvesters,
> Overcome Gods upon Parnassus.[21]

Yeats's rhythmic mastery and lyric voice give just a hint of what could be done with this and other odes of Sophocles.

The deceptively simple Greek must not be turned into an English that is *over*simplified. The odes are deceptively simple precisely because of their gem-like multifaceted beauty, in which the gaze can wonderingly be lost. This is all too often betrayed by translation. Yeats's poem is a beautiful frustration, a shard of a translation we do not have.

The choice of a style of choral translation will inevitably affect the style of choral performance profoundly. Ideal criteria are easy to suggest: a passionate lyric intensity which can handle the change of expressiveness as a chorus enters a choral ode; which is comprehensible without sacrificing the poetical density or emotional complexity of the verse; which is open to performance and the creativity of a director. Easy to suggest such a translation—but hard to find.

Dialogue and Translation

The formal line-by-line exchange of stichomythia can be a nightmare for translators, actors, and directors. Sophocles in particular writes especially multilayered conversations that are incredibly hard to get into an English that works onstage. To try to capture the full sense in a single line often overbloats the timing of the interaction; to cut the lines down results in reducing the dialogue to its lowest common denominator and trivializing the exchange.

I want to look first at two versions of a brief piece of dialogue from Sophocles' *Electra*. I have chosen to look at these two translations because they were used for two productions I have already discussed, each of which was considerably praised by the press and by audiences. It will be instructive to see the differences between two successful translations, and to see what makes up a good version of stichomythia in action. The two productions are Deborah Warner's (with Fiona Shaw and John Lynch) and David Leveaux's (with Zoë Wanamaker and Andrew Howard). The stretch of dialogue is the opening of the recognition scene, as Orestes finds himself unable to keep quiet any longer.

The Warner production used Kenneth McLeish's 1979 translation. They did not make any extensive cuts or changes, but focused in detail on its potential. Here is the passage:

> OR. Now Pylades, what can I say? What words
>   Will help? I can keep silent no more.
> EL. What's the matter? What are you saying, sir?
> OR. Are you really Electra, princess Electra?
> EL. Princess Electra, yes—princess of grief.
> OR. I am sorry for what has happened—
> EL. *You* are sorry? Sorry for whom? For me?
> OR. Treated so cruelly, abandoned by the gods—
> EL. These are words of ill-omen, but they are true.
> OR. Kept without a husband, treated like a slave—
> EL. Sir, we are strangers. Why do you grieve for me?

This was a riveting scene of growing recognition—recognition by Orestes of his sister's state and his own emotional and physical tie to her, and recognition by Electra of the stranger's odd connectedness to her. Sophocles does not specify that Orestes' first line is spoken to Pylades. McLeish has him address his companion (for support? to avoid contact with Electra?), but from Electra's response it is evident that he is turning in his confusion toward her. "What words will help?" is a transition toward an offer of help, and "I can keep silent no more" is sufficiently aimed at Electra to prompt her response. She has recognized his difficulty and asks what is his trouble. Electra is both brilliant at manipulating the rhetoric of others and capable of intense self-absorption. When she recognizes someone else, it matters.

"Are you Electra, princess Electra?" is the question he cannot restrain. "Being oneself" is the crisis every Sophoclean hero and heroine faces. This is a question not just of her ravaged collapse from the pampered status of princess, but of what such a collapse means for her identity. But Electra can rise to the occasion, with an affirmation which buzzes with a typical mixture of pride, sardonic twist, and despair: "Princess Electra, yes—princess of grief." The use of "princess" like this is the translator's wordplay. The Greek has a simpler and evocative "Aye, this is that woman, and so wretched." But the style of Electra's rejoinder in McLeish's version looks back nicely to the sharpness of her self-representation in the arguments with her mother and her sister.

Orestes is quietly struck: "I am sorry for what has happened—" As the dash indicates, this is a half-formed thought. The next two lines also are part of his self-absorbed observation of his sister and reflection on her state. This is a perfect example of what Housman poked fun at, where the genre's expectation of the one line each seems to require unnecessary interruptions by the interlocutor. But Orestes' hesitations are part of his awestruck self-reflection on her state, and Electra's interruptions are no generic requirement. She has been interrupting throughout the play, and here her first remark, "*You* are sorry? For whom? For me?" runs through a gamut of emotions. The first question could almost be funny, but it is perhaps more of a dismissal of what she suspects is shallow sympathy, or a curiosity that anyone could feel for her in her current state. How could this man feel for her?

Orestes, in grim wonder at her suffering, sees her as the victim of man and heaven: "Treated so cruelly, abandoned by the gods—" Sophocles' text actually specifies that her *body* is ravaged disgracefully, godlessly. This was a keynote of Shaw's performance, and the physical signs of her suffering were evident at every moment of the performance. Electra's response is again multivalent. She recognizes the ill omen of the words, not to fend them away in a standard religious gesture, but to accept them as all too applicable to her state. The echo of a normal life, where such ill-omened words should prompt a ritual abjuration, marks how low she has sunk. But Orestes continues with his litany as if her remarks have not been heard in his transfixed stare at Electra: "kept without a husband, treated like a slave—" This is too much for Electra. The third remark on her condition makes her demand a real exchange: "Sir, we are strangers. Why do you grieve for me?" It is an explicit question which requires a response. Electra is directed at Orestes. (In Sophocles, each of her last three remarks is explicitly addressed to Orestes, with a phrase like "O stranger" or "sir": how the characters connect is differently managed.) It is from here that the identification of Orestes starts.

This dialogue is as transparent and clear as McLeish's work usually is. It sticks fairly closely to Sophocles' writing, though the register of McLeish's language is less high-flown than that of Sophocles. But what it achieves excellently is the ebb and flow of emotional connection and disconnection, and the articulation of the space of recognition, self-recognition, and the absorbed observation of the other. McLeish's stichomythia here captures the coming together of two emotionally disturbed and historically connected people.

By way of contrast, here is the version of Frank McGuinness, the Irish writer who also provided the script for the Leveaux/Wanamaker *Electra*, and also later for Jonathan Kent's *Hecuba* starring Clare Higgins.

OR. What can I say?
I cannot speak, but I can no longer hold my tongue.
EL. Why do you say that—what's wrong with you?
OR. Am I looking at the great woman, Electra?
EL. That is me, and I'm a sorry sight.
OR. Yours is a pitiful story. So pitiful.
EL. Sir, your pity is not for me, surely.
OR. Your beauty has been broken and wickedly disfigured.
EL. Yes, sir, I am the woman your words describe.

OR. They stopped you from marrying—they've sentenced you to misery.

EL. Stranger, why do you look at me and lament?[22]

What is fascinating to see here is how the small changes of detail in what is basically the same move toward recognition also change the dynamics of interaction between the two speakers. McGuinness writes strong, pared-down prose, in simple, direct language ("pared down to the very fishbone," as Zoë Wanamaker put it). We have already seen how restricted the role of the chorus is in *Hecuba* and how the choral speaking in *Electra* is reduced to a single confidante of Electra herself. Here the language is stark.

Orestes begins with a stronger paradox than in McLeish's version: "I cannot speak, but I can no longer hold my tongue." There is no Pylades, no gradual turn to Electra, just a struggle with words. It is this struggle which now prompts Electra's "Why do you say that—what's wrong with you?"—a recognition of the almost physical struggle in front of her. When he blurts out his question, "Am I looking at the great woman Electra?" there seems less question of Electra's identity ("Are you really Electra?" [McLeish]) than a focus on the lost and performed greatness of the girl: lost in social terms, but there can be no doubt of her greatness in grief and commitment. Consequently, Electra's affirmation is simpler than in McLeish's version, and closer to Sophocles' Greek: "That is me and I'm a sorry sight."

Orestes expresses his pity for her story. The repetition "so pitiful" is picked up by Electra: "Sir, your pity is not for me, surely." The polite address "sir" is distancing, as is her rejection of his feeling. The "surely" adds a twist at the tail of the sentence. Is she suggesting that his is really a sort of "self-pity"? That his immediate pity is unbelievable to her, suffering as she has over so long? That she is wondering at another human reaching out to her? The sense of distance is maintained in the next exchange. Orestes with an outburst of recognition—it is the longest sentence we have heard for a while in the script— describes why he is indeed pitying, and shocked: "Your beauty has been broken and wickedly disfigured." Orestes does make her disfigurement physical ("Your beauty . . ."), but there is no sense that this is a "godless" act. His blunt statement prompts a little burst of ironic self-affirmation from Electra: "Yes, sir, I am the woman your words describe." Is this resignation? Or a remembrance of once prouder and prettier days, sounding even through her misery? Note that McLeish kept the sense of "ill omen" from Sophocles. This religious undertone has been removed by McGuinness, as it had been removed from Orestes' description of his sister. This is a purely human encounter, without the framing of divine revenge. So where McLeish did not specify a subject for Orestes' next shocked observation ("Kept without a husband, treated like a slave"), McGuinness pointedly refers to Clytemnestra and Aegisthus, though without naming them: "They stopped you from marrying— they've sentenced you to misery." As Orestes comes closer to engaging in the history of the house, Electra pulls back into the question which opens into his recognition: "Stranger, why do you look at me and lament?" The address "stranger," after "sir," marks Electra's recognition of the oddity of his apparently unmotivated grief, and his apparent understanding of the family story, which his use of "they" indicates. It opens a new phase of their interaction.

Both McLeish and McGuinness understand that stichomythia is a taut and rich art form. Each line has no wasted words, but also has enough to provide an actor with a detailed map of contact and discontinuity within the exchange. Each form of address is an act of recognition, each hint of a past or a future narrative is part of the significance of the interaction. In stichomythia no character ever simply says "yes," "no," or "thank you" (the glue of small talk). It is always "yes, because . . . ," or "no, if . . . ," or "thank you, but . . .": every reply takes the conversation on and in a new direction, just as every question drives forward the interaction. A good translation of stichomythia will provide such a detailed emotional and intellectual map. The lines will be densely terse, with a willingness to capture a range of thought and feeling in a small compass, and a strong sense of an unfurling argument. If the lines become too short or pared down, the map becomes featureless; if the lines strive too hard to capture every nuance of the Greek, then the conversation becomes prolix and lacking drive. Yet as we can see from the scripts of McLeish and McGuinness, stichomythia can be an enormous resource for directors and actors, and essential to the dramatic power of Greek tragedy.

Conclusion

A translation is often the starting point of a production, and it will have profound implications for the style of the performance. The choice of the right translation for a company is not a question of which translator gets closest to the Greek original, nor is there one single best translation of any play under all circumstances. Even when a company can commission its own translation, which may develop in rehearsal, it is still always a question of evaluating and balancing often conflicting criteria: the skills required to produce the taut dialogue are not the same as those to create fine choral lyric; great poetry and a great libretto are not the same type of object. One thing is certain, however. The translation really matters, and it is worth some care and attention to get the best one for your production.

I have indicated here some of the general problems of finding an adequate translation, and I have shown in detail some of the instructive solutions and failures of the recent translations that have been used in theaters. So, with all these provisos, can I, finally, recommend a translation? This is, of course, not the place for a full survey of the hundreds of available texts. But perhaps a few pointers on the most familiar plays will help. In each case, I have chosen texts for performance.

For Aeschylus's *Oresteia*, of the productions I have seen, Ted Hughes's translation is the most integrated (though Tony Harrison's has immense strengths, if thoroughly formal, abstract production values are to be adopted). I have not personally seen Robert Fagles's text performed, although it has occasionally been staged in America: it is probably the finest straight literary translation on the market (followed by Robert Lowell's, I suspect, which has also been occasionally performed in the States, usually by university departments). The versions by Peter Meineck and by Alan Shapiro and Peter Burian are intended for theatrical production, but neither has received a full staging yet. Neither, designedly, has the poetic richness of the first three.[23]

For Sophocles, I find Timberlake Wertenbaker's versions in *The Thebans* among the best for her combination of dramatic intensity with lyric flair. Don Taylor's verse translation of *Antigone*, *Oedipus Tyrannus*, and *Oedipus at Colonus* was used for the highly successful BBC TV production of *The Thebans* in 1986, and unlike Raphael and McLeish's *Serpent Son*, it managed to avoid the oppressive naturalism of the medium, and to work both music and lyricism together with a supple and dramatic verse form for the scenic action. It may feel a touch dated nowadays. (Taylor also provided an excellent script for Mitchell's production of Euripides' *Iphigeneia at Aulis* at the National Theatre in London in 2004, with a fine sense of the political language of tragedy in particular.) But it is clear that both Kenneth McLeish's pared-down simplicity and Frank McGuinness's hard intensity are particularly effective with a more naturalistic acting style, especially for the *Electra*. Neither of the two most widely available texts, the David Grene and Richmond Lattimore versions for Chicago and the Penguin Classics of E. F. Watling, is designed for the stage, and neither, rightly, has been much used in performance. For *Antigone*, Seamus Heaney's *Burial at Thebes* plays very well, and has moments of real drive and lyrical softness; *The Cure at Troy* is also a powerful work. There are a great number of translations, particularly of *Oedipus the King* and *Antigone*, available on the open market, many for school and university study, most of which have not been produced professionally (nor will be), going back at least to Sir Richard Claverhouse Jebb's Victorian prose versions. Jebb's stilted, biblical prose will not be staged by any company soon, but if you want to get a good sense of the dry meaning of Sophocles' poetry, Jebb remains a classic resource.[24]

For the most commonly produced Euripidean plays—*Hecuba, Trojan Women, Medea, Hippolytus, Bacchae*—there is also a wealth of teaching translations, but very few successfully produced scripts. Euripides more than Aeschylus and Sophocles has been adapted in the broadest possible ways: *Dionysus in 69*, Richard Schechner's production of the *Bacchae*, is iconic here, but *Medea* too has attracted many new versions which cannot really be called translations, except in the sense that Shakespeare's Bottom is translated.[25] For *Hippolytus*, I have a soft spot for David Rudkin's account, one of few translations by a professional actor. *Medea*, as I have discussed already, has Raphael and McLeish and also Alistair Elliot—two carefully calibrated naturalistic texts. *Hecuba* has a Frank McGuinness translation which has probably the most powerful writing for the lead role, but which unfortunately destroys the choral aspects of the original. Consequently, Timberlake Wertenbaker or Kenneth McLeish is again probably the best bet here. *Trojan Women* has a familiar range: McLeish has been most often produced. The *Bacchae* too has no outstanding script, but for want of something to make the soul sing, Raphael and McLeish again will have to do.[26]

These suggestions are self-consciously conservative: they take texts that have been used by a range of companies, or look likely to last a while. I have not singled out the bold adaptations of Charles Mee, say, or Robert Auletta, or Brendan Kennelly, much as each contains powerful writing.[27] (Nor have I cited the texts I hate or that I find boring.) The continuing popularity of Greek tragedy on the modern stage makes even a brief list such as this inevitably provisional and constantly on the verge of going out of date. It is a cliché that each generation needs to find its own translations, its own response to the power of Greek theater. But much as the acting style of a generation ago can look hilariously mannered, pretentious, or merely slightly outmoded, so too translations are completely of their time. This chapter has outlined the lasting problems that any company will face: new solutions, new excitements, new successes and failures, await.

Chapter Six

Gods, Ghosts, and Helen of Troy

There is nothing more embarrassing in a production of Greek tragedy, professional or amateur, than when an actor with an obviously mortal and aging body dutifully intones, "I am a god . . . ." Like the bar mitzvah boy piping "today I am a man," it seems to invoke no more than the ritual of the occasion. Now we are watching the classics . . . . The need to bring the gods onstage (along with assorted ghosts, heroes, and monsters) can derail any production. In an age of increasingly overwhelming special effects in cinema and other digital media, how can theater represent the gods and monsters which transcend the human, and still make serious and moving drama?

Ghosts, Monsters, and the Face That Launched a Thousand Ships

Before we can look at the representation of the gods themselves on the modern stage, we need first to glance at the ghosts, monsters, and heroes who make up the full range of supernatural beings in tragedy. The gods are part of this more extended cast list.

Hecuba opens with the ghost of Hecuba's murdered son, Polydorus. We looked at his opening words in chapter 3. Ghosts are perhaps the least problematic of the supernatural figures to represent onstage, because there is such a tradition of theatrical ghosts, especially in Shakespeare, where Banquo's ghost—the proverbial ghost at the feast—and the ghost of Hamlet's father have entered the English language as familiar stock expressions. And people still see ghosts. The downside of the familiarity of the ghost in English tragedy is the danger of theatrical cliché—the dry ice and white makeup. Jonathan Kent's *Hecuba* at the Donmar Theatre in 2004, designed by Paul Brown, found a brilliant solution to this problem. There is no curtain at the Donmar; the audience can see the set from the time they take their seats. As the spectators came in, the single singer already occupied her place high on the back wall on her balcony, where she wrote names of the dead and the disappeared on the wall. The stage, with its sand dune, tent flap, and long pool of water were all visible. The dim house lights went down, and then as they came up into a bright full glare, the ghost emerged from the middle of the pool, a tall, gaunt, extremely pale young man, in a white shroud, dripping, from under the water. (Later in the play his body was washed up in the same pool to be discovered by the Trojan prisoners of war.) This was a stunning beginning. The strange appearance of the actor, both his looks and the manner of his entrance, wonderfully evoked the otherworldliness of the ghost. It was technically easy but extremely ingenious to achieve. The pool stretched under the stage area, and from the understage, unseen, of course, to the audience, the actor could simply slip into the pool, dive down and rise before the audience. But the imaginative effect was truly impressive.

Two other Greek tragic ghosts make regular appearances. In Aeschylus's *Persians*, the ghost of Darius, the father of King

Xerxes, whose disastrous expedition against Greece the play celebrates, appears in order to make judgment on his son from the underworld. Here, the ghost is conjured up by the chorus and queen through magic ritual and song from the tomb on-stage. This is a scene designed for spectacle—weird Eastern rites, a splendidly dressed and authoritative kingly spirit, a judgment from the grave. The extended ritual performance both motivates the appearance of the ghost—unlike the deus ex machina or the sudden appearance of Polydorus—and also provides a special frame for the ghost's representation. Again, the parallels with Shakespearean spirits and his love of pageant from the other world, help make this scene easily assimilated by a modern audience. The visions in *Macbeth* or *Julius Caesar* give obvious parallels, and the immense variety of productions of those plays offers a range of potential staging techniques.

Clytemnestra's appearance as a ghost in the *Eumenides* is more complex. She appears as part of the complex rush of short scenes which open the third play of the *Oresteia* and bring onstage the full range of divine beings. The play begins with a priestess praying to the gods of Delphi. She enters the shrine, and then comes out on all fours, screaming, terrified, from what she has seen inside—the Furies. She describes them for us, as snoring, suppurating, dark, and terrifying females, like Gorgons. ("Dark, dank, and disgusting. / Their foul stench and hideous breath forced me back, / and their eyes seep a repulsive, putrid pus," as Peter Meineck's translation puts it.)[1] Then Apollo, the purifying god of Delphi himself, emerges with Orestes, to send him on his way to Athens. As Orestes exits, the ghost of Clytemnestra enters to rouse the chorus of Furies to chase him. They awake, and rush in only to be dismissed from the holy site by the god with the threat of his bow and arrows. They pursue Orestes to Athens—where the rest of the play is set. The stagecraft here—the swiftness of change of scene, of entrance and exit of characters, and the sheer variety of figure and interaction—is unparalleled in Greek tragedy. In the *Libation Bearers* it seemed that seeing the Furies was a sign of Orestes' mad flight from the scene of matricide. Now, ghosts, gods, and Furies are all onstage, visible to all, and leading players in the drama. There is a shift in level of representation, which will continue, as these figures become the courtroom debaters before a jury of Athenian citizens. Clytemnestra's ghost is part of this world full of gods.

The appearance of the terrifying but now murdered Clytemnestra is conceptually easy to place within this world full of gods. But how she is represented is part and parcel of a far more difficult problem: the characterization of the Furies and the Olympian gods, within this most politically charged of plays. The Furies in this scene provide perhaps the most tricky moment of representation in all of Greek tragedy. A story from the ancient world tells us that their first entrance was so terrifying that women in the theater had miscarriages. The story comes only from a very late source (from a time when women were regular theatergoers), but it does indicate that the Priestess's shocked reaction is a guide for the audience.[2] What sort of an appearance should the Furies make? In ancient Greece itself, the Furies are usually represented as rather elegant winged females who carry torches (fig. 13). They dance or fly around a victim, and through their voices and expressions throw his mind into confusion. The Priestess specifies that the Furies she sees are without wings, and her description adds the disturbing physical details of stench and oozing to the standard painted image. This type of image of the Furies continues into the nineteenth century. Figure 14 is Bouguereau's famous picture of Orestes being hunted by the Furies. They carry the corpse of his mother, with the blood freshly running, and swirl around the hero, who covers his ears in terror. It is the sound as much as the sight of the Furies that terrifies him. They are naked from the waist, and the leading Fury's face is distorted in aggressive rage, as she

13 A fourth-century vase showing Orestes beset by two Furies, who carry snakes and burning torches. Orestes is, typically for Greek heroes, nude, and tries to ward off the Furies with his sword and scabbard.

wields a torch. The fear of women out of control seems to run through this image. Bouguereau himself may have been instrumental in opening the atelier to female artists, but this is very much a Victorian male portrait of how the female might terrify the imagination.

Modern productions have not rejected this image of the Furies entirely, though it has been used only with drastic adaptation to contemporary cultural ideas. The American Repertory Theatre put on the *Oresteia* in Cambridge, Massachusetts, in 1994 with a translation by Robert Auletta, directed by François Rochaix, and with costumes by Catherine Zuber. The Furies appeared as if nearly naked (though body stockings were worn), with tattoos of twisting snakes, and other tribal markings (fig. 15). With short-cropped blond

14 Bouguereau's *Orestes Pursued by the Furies* (1862): Orestes cowers and tries to cover his ears from the bitter words of the chasing Furies.

hair, they look like demonized chorus dancers from an interwar Berlin nightclub, especially when they drink to the new deal agreed with the gods. This appearance strives to redesign the old image of the half-naked, swirling, aggressive Furies into a modern style of cultural anxiety, hoping to capture something of the sense of being out of control, wild, and a threat. The production unfortunately was not a great success, partly because it played the *Eumenides* for laughs—which inevitably worked against any fear or awe that the Furies might inspire.

Ariane Mnouchkine adopted a quite different approach in *Les Atrides*. She split her chorus into two leaders of the chorus (choruphaioi) and a collection of chorus members. The two leaders were dressed like rough tramps or bag ladies, with

15 The ghost of Clytemnestra and the Furies from the American Repertory Theatre's *Oresteia*, directed by François Rochaix. Tattoos of snakes recall the snakes of earlier images of the Furies (see figs. 12 and 13), and female nudity—or, here, body stockings to represent nudity—is used as a threat.

dirty, ill-fitting costumes, dusty white faces, and disheveled hair. They carried sticks, and reacted with verve and force to the scenes unfolding around them. They were accompanied by a chorus of baboon-like creatures with large masks, who crawled and jabbered and barked around the stage (fig. 16). This combined an imagination of bourgeois fear of urban violence with a sense of animalistic physicality. This imagery fitted well with the political understanding of the play provided by the translator, Hélène Cixous, who sees the Furies as the product of the patriarchal imagination, here tinged by her distaste for bourgeois ideals. The contrast between the Furies and Athene and Apollo was particularly striking. Athene was shimmering in whiteness and purity, and with calm, elegant movement and established, authoritative presence. Again, the play's conceptual contrasts were strongly expressed by the costume and the bodies of the actors.

16 A Fury and the two leaders of the chorus of Furies from Mnouchkine's *Les Atrides*. The idea of bag ladies with wild dogs draws on contemporary bourgeois urban fears.

Yet neither Mnouchkine's nor the American Repertory Theatre's Furies could really be called frightening or awe-inspiring. Have other companies been able to summon a real sense of fear or disgust? Peter Hall's production at the National Theatre in 1981 had bare-faced masks, white with gaping eyes and mouth, with a shock of red ringlets (fig. 17). The blankness became menacing when tied to words and movements (though some verses of Harrison's binding song were less successful than others: "Show us your hands. Left. Right. / You'll live unhunted if they're white"). Yet these masks were also quite closely similar in appearance to the masks of the main characters, and there was little physical sense that they were disgustingly different from Athene or Electra.

Peter Stein directed the *Oresteia* twice. In his second production with a Russian company and Russian translation, which opened in Moscow in the midst of the shattering political changes of the 1990s (before playing in an ice-rink at the

17 Orestes and the chorus of Furies from the Peter Hall/Tony Harrison *Oresteia*. The blank faces bring some terror, but the image is also carefully aestheticized by its formal balletic movement.

Edinburgh Festival), his female chorus were dressed in discarded military jackets under which were the black undergarments of the housewife of the old Soviet period. At the end of the play, the Furies were garlanded to mark their assimilation into the city, but this garlanding turned into a sort of swaddling, binding the Furies in place. This image of repressive control (with the threat of future explosion out of the chrysalis) made a powerfully ironic political comment on the new freedoms of the state—and contrasted strongly with Stein's first performance in the 1980s (fig. 18), where the play optimistically celebrated the potential of progress in the state (though with a chorus of Furies of frog-like monstrosity). Stein also played the later *Eumenides* with a raucous, ironic humor (perhaps the only adequate response to Soviet politics), and here too the chorus lacked awe and fearsomeness, though the final image made its political point with chilling visual authority.

18 The Furies and Athena from Peter Stein's production of the *Oresteia* in Berlin. The Furies' faceless monstrosity contrasts significantly with the white simplicity and open face of the goddess. Behind them stand the jurors of the trial of Orestes, with the voting pebbles on the desk to the right.

Horror and science fiction films have changed a modern audience's perception of the physically grotesque and the frightening. This makes the representation of the Furies on-stage doubly difficult, and none of the shows discussed above can be said to have successfully achieved a combination of the fearsome and the awesome. It is especially hard to create an image from the traditional representations of out-of-control and physically transgressive females: wild hair, painted faces, and seminaked bodies are more likely to recall *The Rocky Horror Picture Show* than a religiously led fear of punishment. The more that the representation of the Furies is historically located (Soviet housewives, suicide bombers), the less easy it is for them to tap into the religious dimension of their role; the more abstract their representation (faceless, pregnant women, wild haired harridans, frog-like monsters), the more difficult it is to evoke fear and awe. The Furies need to uncover a dangerously unpleasant physicality in their performance, and this cannot rely on costume alone. But for a modern audience the link between horror and physical form is often distasteful: it is unlikely to be thought acceptable to use images of physical disablement or the female body itself to indicate disgust or fear. To find a modern image that uncovers a fearsome bestiality and vengeful violence within a female form is a real challenge today. It is not as though such visceral terrors have disappeared from society. We await the Furies for the twenty-first century.

The Furies are hard to represent partly because they are an extreme category: female, divine, monstrous, violent. This is also true of the semidivine figures who appear in several plays, and who are important precisely because they go so far beyond the limits of normal humans. Heracles appears in several plays. In *Alcestis* (most recently translated by Ted Hughes),[3] he arrives at the house of Admetus after Admetus's wife, Alcestis, has been taken off by Death (she is the only one of Admetus's family who is prepared to die in his place). Heracles, indebted to Admetus, will wrestle Death, defeat him, and bring Alcestis back to the living world to marry Admetus again. Heracles is a figure to wrestle Death and win. In *The Women of Trachis* he is the great conquering hero who has rid the world of monsters, but who is in the play destroyed by the poisoned robe sent to him by his wife. He is as huge and overbearing in his grief and pain as he is in his warlike labors. In *The Mad Heracles*, he returns home in the nick of time to save his wife (a different one) and their children from the clutches of an evil tyrant, only to be sent mad by the goddess Hera in the second half of the play, when he slaughters his whole family. Again, the savior turned murderer embodies the duality of this figure who is (as Aristotle put it), "the best of men and the worst of men for his appetites." In *Philoctetes*, he is now the divine hero Heracles, who appears at the end of the play to direct his former friend and colleague Philoctetes toward a cure and glory on the battlefield.[4]

In all of these plays, Heracles is a larger-than-life figure. He is described as physically huge. His desires are consuming. Like all heroes, he is both a potential savior and a dangerous threat, even to the same people. He is a rapist and looter who cleanses the world of evil. His pain is earth-shaking. His strength transcends death, and he is the one human who becomes a divinity, and he ends in most stories marrying the goddess Hebe (Prime of Life) and living on Mount Olympus. For later Greeks, he even became a paradigm of philosophical thinking as well as the prime example of virtue. Figure 19 is a Roman image of Heracles, the so-called Farnese Heracles found in the Baths of Caracalla in Rome. It shows how the body of Heracles can be imagined in the ancient world. Swollen with muscles, but reflectively gazing down, he epitomizes an athletic combination of the training of body and mind. The statue is over eight feet tall. This is a big man, big enough to wrestle death.

Heracles repeatedly transcends the limitations of the human body whether in raping fifty women in one night or holding the earth on his shoulders to give Atlas a rest. It puts a good deal of pressure on any actor who is to play Heracles. In ancient tragedy, actors could use raised boots (usually called "buskins"), large masks, and splendid costumes—though even here we have jokes about small men who cannot live up to the name of Heracles. But it is certainly possible for an actor with real stage presence and physical stature to make a role. Martin Crimp, a fine young playwright who has worked with the Complicite company, one of the most exciting theatrical groups in Europe, wrote *Cruel and Tender*, which was produced at the Young Vic in London in 2004 (directed by Luc Bondy). It is a reworking of Sophocles' *Women of Trachis*, with the Heracles figure called "The General" (played by Joe Dixon). The attempt here was to locate Heracles' status not in

19 The Farnese Heracles: the muscle-bound
hero, destined for divinity.

size, but rather in power and in lethal violence. The sense of
military strength, and above all physical dominance, was conveyed through the physical and authoritative bearing—overbearing—of the General. When he appears later crushed by
his sickness, the tensions within the characterization of Heracles in Sophocles' play found powerful modern expression. It
inevitably played down the divine and supernatural elements
of Sophocles' plot, but it made for a fine and moving drama.

Helen of Troy brings different worries. She is, of course,
the most beautiful woman in the world. Her father is Zeus,

king of the gods: she is not wholly human. She is so beautiful that every man who sees her desires her (and her history
is a long series of rapes and abductions: as Aeschylus puts it,
she is "a woman of many men"). Euripides in particular puts
Helen onstage, in his plays *Helen*, *Orestes*, and, especially, *Trojan Women*. In the *Trojan Women* she is brought on to argue for
her life, with her cuckolded husband Menelaus as judge and
jury, and, as prosecution, Hecuba, the queen of the city of
Troy, which had been destroyed in order to win Helen back. It
is a fabulous scene. Helen argues with great intellectual verve
and wit that she can't be blamed for her adultery since a god
made her do it. Her ultratrendy and flashy rhetoric manipulates the well-known myth that the goddess Aphrodite gave
Helen to Paris as his prize for choosing her as the most beautiful goddess. She also accuses Hecuba herself: she had been
sent an omen that Paris would be the destruction of Troy,
and instead of killing him, she sent him as a shepherd into
the mountains (where he judged the goddesses). It was, says
Helen, Hecuba's error in ignoring the omen that led to Troy's
fall. Hecuba retorts with a passionate rationalism. Helen may
claim a god made her do it, but that is just a rhetorical blind
for her own lust. She caused the war by committing adultery
and running off. She lusted after Eastern men and Eastern
wealth and luxury. She should be put to death. After hearing
both speeches, Menelaus agrees that Hecuba is right and that
Helen should be executed. He will take her home to Greece
and kill her there as an example for all Greek women. Hecuba
is appalled and begs Menelaus not to let her on his ship. He
fails to see her worry. But she knows—and so do we—that
on ship he will fall for her all over again, and that Helen will,
as always, live happily ever after. Indeed, Helen comes to her
trial dressed to the nines, while Hecuba is in the rags of a
prisoner-of-war camp. Menelaus is falling for Helen even
now. The most beautiful woman in the world is so beautiful
she can use any argument and still win over her man. Eurip-

ides is provocatively asking his democratic audience what is more persuasive: rational argument or desires and passions. There is, as ever, a profoundly serious political point within the flashy theatrical brilliance of the staged debate.[5]

Not only does the scene bring onstage the most beautiful woman in the world, but the dynamics of the scene depend on her seductiveness and Menelaus's weakness before her beauty. Casting—and dressing—Helen is not easy. She acts as if she were a human in her seductive performance and rhetorical stance—like Hecuba—yet is more than merely human in her beauty and in its effect on those around her. Two of the most recent professional productions I have seen both chose to make Helen into a Marilyn Monroe, with her characteristic blond curls, tight dress, and red lipstick.[6] Marilyn Monroe is sexy, famous, and instantly recognizable to any audience, and no doubt seductive ("Happy Birthday, Mr. Menelaus"). Yet this slightly vulgar modern allusion also brought with it a host of unwelcome associations (from dumb blond to murder victim) as well as a historical specificity that distorted the argument's dynamics. It is fascinating that no Greek text—and there are many that talk about Helen—ever describes her. Roland Barthes, the great French critic, famously said that you cannot describe beauty: you can only give similes ("lovely as a Madonna") or tautologies ("the perfect smile").[7] But for Helen there is not even any attempt at itemization ("blond hair, blue eyes"). The Greek texts know well that perfect beauty is in the mind of the beholder, the imagination of the lover. A director who had the confidence *not* to show Helen's face, or to have her alone without a mask in a masked production, might be able to get the sense of a beauty so extreme that it is a different kind from ordinary female loveliness. Which woman, after all, could fulfill or transcend the fantasies of the theater audience?

What makes staging Helen, Heracles, and the Furies so difficult is that each is an extreme figure, physically as well as morally. Each goes beyond the norms of human life. Each in his or her own way—through beauty, physical strength, physical horror—takes us to the limit of the imagination, and that is why the representation of these figures will always be so challenging. This extremism is crucial to the roles they play in any drama in which they appear. So, the insistent problem a director faces with these figures can be expressed succinctly: how to construct a convincing form of representation which transcends the world of the human actors?

Getting the Gods Onstage

The difficulty of staging the gods can be expressed in three main ways. First, the ancient Greek range of expectation is inevitably hugely different from a modern audience's cultural norms. The Greek audience were usually educated in Homer as well as in their own polytheistic religious practices.[8] In the epics of Homer, there are scenes set on Mount Olympus where the gods debate the course of the war at Troy, decide to intervene in the events on earth, and enjoy drinking, sex, eating, and arguing. On the battlefields of the *Iliad*, or in the course of Odysseus's journey home in the *Odyssey*, gods appear repeatedly, usually in disguise, and engage fully in the human action. Not only do they fill heroes with strength and cunning, but also they are wounded by mortals, they are complained to, and in turn they tease their human favorites. The divinities are represented in anthropomorphic form—like bigger, stronger, more beautiful humans; they appear to humans often disguised as humans; and they directly engage with humans.

These epics gave the Greeks their idea of the gods (as the ancient historian Herodotus states);[9] and in a religious context gods are represented by statues, also in anthropomorphic form, and in both hero cults and elsewhere gods are said to appear to humans. Epiphany—the sudden appearance of a god in mundane life—is part of religious experience. The direct interaction of gods and humans—which is often brutal, cruel, and apparently unfair—challenges the expectations of a modern Western audience, and causes an immediate problem when contemporary drama seeks to represent the gods onstage. We just can't share the ancient preconceptions built into the texts of Greek tragedy that gods will appear and interact with humans. It is distinctly troubling to modern regimes of thought when we see the body of a god or goddess too closely. We do not like gods to have sex with humans. We do not like gods happily to destroy innocent people in their pursuit of revenge. For a modern audience, schooled to believe that god is "immortal, invisible, God only wise," the Greek divinities are bound to be a challenge.

Second, there is always when staging the gods the danger of—to put it bluntly—ridiculousness. This is particularly pressing with the deus ex machina. There are many occasions in Greek tragedy when the deus ex machina arrives which can strike a modern audience in a comical way. ("I simply had not the nerve to bring on a god two minutes from curtain," confesses Seamus Heaney.)[10] Euripides' play *Orestes* was one of the most popular plays in antiquity. In its final scene, Orestes is on the roof of Menelaus's palace with Electra and Pylades. He has his sword to the throat of Menelaus's daughter, and he has already murdered Helen of Troy. The palace is on fire. A Phrygian eunuch has fled from the palace singing a terrified song. Menelaus is approaching the palace with an army to retake it. At this point, it would appear that the chaos in the expected narratives of myth is as great as the chaos onstage. How can Orestes kill Helen or Menelaus's daughter? Enter Apollo. He tells Orestes not to kill that girl, but marry her; announces that Helen of Troy has not been killed after all, but become a star; sends Menelaus home. And tidies everything into a neat mythic parcel.

The contrast between the human confusion with its conflicting emotions and motivations and the god's arbitrary reorganization of the events of the story is startling. It is also typical of Euripides, who loves to write plays that have strong endings that are nonetheless full of worries and doubts for the audience. But for modern spectators, the appearance of a god who just says "no" and restructures the plot is likely to provoke amusement and/or annoyance. Not only is the audience's relation to the gods obviously different from what we might expect in an ancient culture—these are not our gods, after all—but also our expectations of a well-made play are influenced by generations of criticism and drama writing. This tradition has made the deus ex machina seem like the archetypal theatrical convention to get a plot out of a hole that has been dug for it. The reaction of the modern audience to the appearance of Heracles in Heaney's *The Cure at Troy*, when I saw it in London, was exactly this: a benevolent but slightly mocking smile or laugh, as the hero duly arrived to sort out the impossible mess of the human plot. The irruption of the gods onstage often marks a crisis, a moment of redefinition or redirection. But for this reason it always runs the risk of seeming like a comically arbitrary device of playwrights.

This leads directly to the third worry, which I can sum up in the single word "staginess." As with the acting style in which declamation is necessary for Greek tragedy, so the appearance of a god can act as a sign of being in the theater. When the audience becomes too aware that "this is a stage effect," or "this is an actor," the danger for the performance is that the spectators disengage from the scene. In *Chorus Line*, the disembodied voice of the director, spoken over the microphone, makes sense because it is rooted in the theatrical practice of the audition. When the gods are played by a disembodied voice in the theater—an option repeatedly taken—because "god's voice" has no adequate rooting in Greek or modern culture, the risk is that it is undermined by its own evident staginess.

]]] [[[

So how have contemporary directors approached the problem of the gods? I have returned in this book so far to a restricted number of plays. This is partly because modern theater has repeatedly chosen to restage a limited selection of the surviving plays. There are no doubt many reasons why *Antigone* has been played so many times since the nineteenth century, and George Steiner has written a fine book detailing how this work speaks to the politics and cultural concerns of modernity with a particularly powerful voice.[11] It is crucial to this popularity that *Antigone* has no gods in it. This absence is integral to the effect of the drama: it is a play about humans in conflict, each of whom can appeal to the (silent) gods in different and selectively polemical ways. The lack of a god's authoritative voice is central to this play's refusal to allow its audience a simple route through its moral conflicts. It also makes it an attractive play for modern companies, because it does not need to face the problem of staging the gods.

Of Sophocles' seven surviving plays, only the *Ajax* has a divinity onstage, and even then the script specifies that Odysseus can only hear the voice of Athene (and not see her). This absence of a god onstage may have helped contribute to the popularity in recent years of Sophocles' *Electra*, *Oedipus the King*, and *Oedipus at Colonus*, which have featured prominently in the earlier chapters of this book. The same is true for Euripides. From his varied output, the two most popular plays are probably *Medea* and *Hecuba*, neither of which has a divinity in it. One answer to the question of how to stage the gods is to select one of the plays which does not require the visible presence of a divinity onstage. It has proven a particularly popular answer in contemporary theater.

Even when the gods do not appear physically, however, the language of Greek tragedy is full of the religion of Athens. There is no play where the characters do not talk of, refer to, and debate the role of divinities. Translations respond differently to this. We have already seen how McLeish and McGuinness dealt with the suggestion that the treatment of Electra was somehow a sign of godlessness. McLeish emphatically writes "abandoned by the gods"; McGuinness removes any sense of the divine with "wickedly disfigured." This contrast is paradigmatic. There are versions which are happy to dot their texts with references to god or the gods, and to mention gods by name, and other translations which play down any reference to the gods wherever possible, and, in particular, soften or simply cut the language of myth.

The choices here at one level may seem clear-cut. On one side of the argument it is obvious that regular reference to the gods is part of a coherent world picture of a culture in which the gods play an integral and expected role. Many plays have central passages which turn on the rhetoric of the divine. So in *Antigone* when the guard comes in to report the burial of Polyneices, he suggests it may be the hand of god at work. Creon dismisses him out of hand:

> Enough. Don't anger me. Your age, my friend,
> Still doesn't give you rights to talk such garbage.
> The gods, you think, are going to attend
> To this particular corpse? Preposterous.
> Did they hide him under clay for his religion?
> For coming to burn their colonnaded temples?
> For attacking a city under their protection?
> The gods, you think, will side with the likes of him?

Creon (here in Seamus Heaney's muscular verse)[12] not only dismisses the thought that the gods would support the traitor Polyneices, but also goes on snarlingly to find human rebels to be the probable cause for the burial. Talking of the divine in tragedy is often part of such arguments, where characters appeal to the gods as part of a claim of how the world is. It is—simply—an essential element in the rhetoric of persuasion and the challenge of explanation in Greek culture. Creon will in due time be forced by Teiresias to recognize the gods' interest in pollution. Here, his political reasoning uses the gods as part of his forceful argument. Antigone in turn will claim she is following the gods' immutable law in burying her brother—and die for her commitment to it. Other references to the gods in surrounding speeches support and reinforce this central dynamic of the conflict in the *Antigone*. In the twenty-first century, where religion is a central force in the most violent conflicts of society, Greek tragedy's fascination with extremism and the rhetoric of divine support should strike a chillingly familiar note.

But—and here is the other side of the argument—the names of ancient mythology are difficult for a modern audience, and if they need constant explanation, the play becomes a museum or school piece rather than a drama. As Antigone marches to her death, the chorus sing a lyric comparing her to other figures in myth. They give three examples, Danae; the son of Dryas (that is, Lycurgus); and Cleopatra, the daughter of the wind god Boreas and wife of Phineus (nothing to do with Egypt and Elizabeth Taylor). The language is densely allusive, even for a modern scholar. Heaney is more generous than most and does write a few lines on Danae, who "too was walled up in the dark," before being visited by Zeus in a shower of gold—the one part of the story that might be familiar to his audience. But all the other references are cut, as in most modern versions. The original production of Heaney's translation (Dublin, 2004) rained sand and dirt down on Antigone as these lines were delivered. The contrast between the glorification of Danae in a shower of gold, and Antigone's humiliation in the earth was dramatically embodied. Heaney manages to link Antigone's death into the world of myth, in the words and action. Many productions understandably cut every complex reference to ancient myth.

One of the ways that tragedy becomes more than a localized story is through the constant interweaving of its stories with the tapestry of myth that stretches back in time and across the Greek landscape. It revels in the names and stories that people the Greek imagination. The less that modern audiences come with an education which has introduced them to such figures, the more a modern production has to cut or try to explain. Take the *Oresteia*. The pull and threat of the past is a constant and ominous presence in the script: an audience does need to know who Thyestes and Atreus are, not least since they are referred to often. What should a production do? Can a script become more revealing without becoming naïvely expository? When lines are added to the text, it can feel horribly clunky ("Thyestes, Aegisthus's father, who had sex with the wife of Atreus, Agamemnon's father, which explains the conflict in the current generation between Aegisthus, who has sex with Agamemnon's wife, Clytemnestra . . ."). This sort of exposition is also quite unlike the *Oresteia*'s language elsewhere. So many productions turn to the program and give a plot précis with background. But is a program note enough? Don't family trees in programs just exacerbate the sense of alienation and ignorance? The detailed preparation of a script for production needs to explore carefully how the language of myth and the invocation of the gods is an integral part of the performance. The best translations manage to combine density and clarity of exposition where necessary, and the ability to evoke a broader landscape from a few words.

Even when a play is chosen which does not bring gods onstage, the text of the play will be full of god talk, and interwoven with the repertoire of myth. Finding the right level of this religious discourse is a difficult but necessary task; a production has to negotiate a space between recognizing that the mythology and appeals to the divine are an essential dynamic of the play's moral and rhetorical structure, and recognizing that a modern audience is likely to be baffled by or alienated from

such language. Thinking about how the gods are to be represented is not merely a question of how to put an actor onto the
stage. The language of the play throughout frames any direct
appearance of a divinity, and when a translation presents confident and controlled god talk, the staging of the supernatural
forces becomes a far less jarring and difficult event.

Face to Face with the Gods

In the ancient theater, the sense of the special plane of the
gods was achieved in three main ways. First and most simply,
the gods appeared *ex machina*, on the crane which allowed
them to fly above the stage and the audience. Second, they
appeared on the *theologeion*, the god-walk at the top of the
stage building (though humans also appeared there on occasion, as we saw in chapter 1). The spatial dynamics of the
theater created a sense of physical transcendence and separate
spheres for gods and humans. Third, costume and style of
speech separated the divine and the mortal. Gods were recognized by the splendor of their robes, the traditional markers
of their identity (Athene's aegis, Apollo's bow, and so forth),
and by their authoritative pronouncements, especially in the
prologues and epilogues of plays. But let us look at how these
ancient resources can—or cannot—become part of a modern
dramatic language.

Let us once again begin with Aeschylus. The *Oresteia*, one
of the most produced of all ancient dramas in recent years,
offers quite different circumstances for the representation of
the gods onstage from all the other plays we will be considering. As we have already mentioned in this chapter, the first
two plays of the trilogy return obsessively to the relationship
between man and god—divine explanations for the action,
Cassandra's prophecies, fear of divine punishment, hymns
and prayers to gods. But no god appears onstage. In the third
play of the trilogy, the *Eumenides*, in the first scene Apollo, the

Furies and the ghost of Clytemnestra are all visible and taking forceful part in the action. From here on, the gods play a major role. They are not on the theologeion or the crane, but acting on the stage and interacting with the humans. Apollo, the Furies, and Athene all participate in the trial, and the relationship between the gods is as important as the relationship between the mortals and the immortals. In the *Oresteia*, finally the gods walk the world amid humans, and in many ways the humans are the observers or victims of their action: the silent jurors vote (and set their city at risk); Orestes is threatened with destruction by the vengeful Furies. But it is the speeches of the Furies, Athene, and Apollo on which the play turns.

The question facing a production of the *Oresteia* is not how to create the separate spheres of divine and human world, but how to integrate them, while making sense of the immortal figures. We have just seen how Ariane Mnouchkine represents her chorus of Furies, and how she set them in very deliberate contrast with the goddess Athene, and the god Apollo, who was also dressed in shimmering white. He "flew" around the set, leaping with great agility to the heights of the walls. Between the urban riffraff and bestial monstrosity of the chorus, and the gilded beauty of the gods, was Orestes, whose simpler black trousers and white shirt distinguished him both from the gods and from the Furies. The costumes and the physical action created a map, a schematization of man, beast, and god, with man caught between the gods above him and the beasts below. The female Furies were firmly of the lower world; Athene clearly above. The categories of the *Oresteia* were beautifully articulated, for all that the characters occupied the same physical space and interacted through it.

The design of Mnouchkine's production, with its resistance to any claims of realism, was part and parcel of the success of this strategy of representation. The *Eumenides'* staging of the gods seems inevitably to resist naturalistic drama in a modern theater. The American Repertory Theatre's *Oresteia*, whose

20 The final scene of the *Oresteia* directed by François Rochaix for the American Repertory Theatre. The gods rise above the Furies, who stand above a representation of Athens itself, brightly lit—creating a tableau to capture the ideological significance of the end of the trilogy.

mockery of the divine undercut the performance of the last play, did end with one particularly powerful image (fig. 20). The gods are at the top of this tableau, Apollo, Athene, and Hermes. They are posed like a statue group from the ancient world and the iconography is markedly neoclassical (except for Hermes' sneakers, a rather grotesque Warholian touch), in a way that belies the costuming elsewhere. At the middle level are the Furies, with their very different style of costuming. Below them, at the level of the stage floor, or the audience, is a glowing model of the Acropolis. The final procession of women has left for the Acropolis singing praises of the city whose citadel the Acropolis is. This final tableau creates a fine spatial map. The gods are above everything, in a calm and stately poise. Below them in awkward stasis are caught the Furies, aggressive protectors of justice, now like a line of caryatids or soldiers. They are above the idealized image of the city whose laws they are to protect. The city is, precisely, a model. This last tableau, like sculptures on a temple, polemically and intelligently projects a notion of the ideology of order at the close of this trilogy.

The gods of the *Oresteia* have been talked about for two plays before they appear. When they appear, they take a full part in the action. In many ways, and especially with the drive toward stylization that has dominated stagings of the *Oresteia* in the last eighty years, this makes staging the gods easier, because they are already so integrated into the drama. Yet there is also a need for differentiation onstage between the categories of the gods, the Furies, and the human—through costume, status, space, lighting, and so forth. I have resisted making too dogmatic statements about what plays (must) mean. But I will here say that I think that the wish to play the *Eumenides* as satire or comedy is not only a desperate response to the problem of the shift of register of these plays, where the gods become visible, but also a failure to understand the seriousness of the political ideas—and ideals—of this third play, which emerge from and are deeply interconnected with the turmoil of the first two tragedies of the trilogy. This inability to see how seriously the *Oresteia* takes democracy, the politics of conflict, and the notion of divine order will prevent the play from having political impact in a contemporary context, where such values remain the source of dissension and hope for so many people.

Euripides treats divine figures quite differently from Aeschylus, and his plays bring to light quite different problems in staging the gods. Euripides is instrumental in developing the divine prologue and epilogue as formal aspects of drama. The *Oresteia* begins with a watchman waiting for a beacon light in the darkness. All of Sophocles' plays begin in the midst of action: *Antigone* with the two sisters plotting in the half light of dawn, for example; or *Electra* with Orestes and the Tutor checking over their plan of revenge; *Oedipus the King* with Oedipus's first great political address. But several of Euripides' plays begin with a god (and sometimes a human) talking, apparently to the audience, sometimes even outlining the setting and the action to come. This is the origin of what will become a formalized part of the dramatic tradition, so that Shakespeare's *Romeo and Juliet* can begin with a character called, simply, "Prologue," who tells the audience what's what.

The formal divine prologue is especially hard to stage, but understanding its dramatic effect will help one see its potential. First of all, the formal prologue separates the god from the human action. The gods will not have direct contact with the humans onstage (as in the *Oresteia*), nor will they appear to humans. Yet the gods can have a determinative effect on the action. When humans discuss how the divine world affects them, they do so as if in a vacuum: they can deny the gods, wrangle about the gods, pray to the gods. But for the audience who has also seen the prologue, these interactions are constantly framed by the knowledge of what the gods have said and done.

This produces some extraordinary ironies. Take *Trojan Women*, for example. The prologue of this play is a conversation between Athene and Poseidon, god of the sea. Athene explains that she has been insulted by the Greek treatment of her religious sites during the sack of Troy and she wants the Greeks to be shipwrecked on their journey home. Poseidon, a god who has supported Troy throughout the conflict, is amazed at the change of attitude of Athene, who has always supported the Greek cause. But he agrees, as god of the sea, to stir up a storm to scatter and shatter the Greek fleet. The prologue shows us the gods as moving forces in human action; it shows them also as fickle and aggressive; and it establishes the principle of reversal: those who are victors will become victims. Because of the prologue, the Greek self-confidence in their triumph is undermined from the beginning. But when

Hecuba and Helen argue about the causes of the Trojan war, and Hecuba argues that Helen uses the excuse of a god's will to excuse her own lust, and that in fact gods do not take such a part in human events, her rational and persuasive argument is also undercut by the prologue, where we have seen precisely such engagement by the gods in human activities. The prologue sets the gods apart in a separate world, but actively, violently impinging on human life; the humans onstage argue whether or how the gods are involved with their activities. The prologue in this way gives dramatic form to the ideas and ironies of the tragedy.

But it also creates huge problems for a modern director. The *Trojan Women* is a play full of human sufferings and the desperate attempts and failures of consolation in the aftermath of war. The power of this portrayal of women on the edge has attracted generations of directors and writers. Yet the play has to start somewhere else, in a different register altogether (unless a modern adaptation without any divine frame is adopted). It is easy to see that a production needs to create a world apart, yet connected, to the mortal woes, but it has proven far more difficult for modern productions to achieve that aim (for all the technical possibilities of lights and sets). I have seen attempts to play the gods as talk-show hosts (no doubt as an image of power and fickleness), as children (emphasizing the danger of power in fickle hands), of large shadows on a wall with a voiceover (inscrutable authority). The gimmickry of each staging stood against the action that followed rather than establishing a frame for it. More successfully, Liz Diamond's production at the Oregon Shakespeare Festival in 2000 had Athene in a severe business suit and trench coat, Poseidon also in a trench coat, with different lighting from the rest of the play, and with the human characters frozen onstage. A separate world and a world of power was strikingly evoked (as was the world-weary and dismissive attitude of the Olympian gods toward mere mortals). I mentioned in passing in chapter 3 how the size of some of the roles in Greek tragedy can cause specific problems: here is a paradigmatic case. Although figures of real presence and stature are needed both for the particular roles and to open the play with authority, both divinities appear onstage for only a few minutes and, in Athene's case, speak a mere twenty-five lines. What's more, as we saw with the *Hecuba* prologue, this is a scene that is entered cold. There is no buildup to the entrance of the divine (as in the *Oresteia*), no motivation for the entrance (as with Darius's ghost or the Furies). Each scene of the *Trojan Women* brings its technical challenges, but this prologue seems to me to be in fact the hardest scene of the play to make work. The prologue demonstrates vividly just how difficult it can be to present the gods on the modern stage.

The divine epilogue or deus ex machina is also associated with Euripidean theater in particular, and has a long subsequent history. We have already discussed how Apollo arrives in the *Orestes* to sort out the plot as it appears to be careering off its mythic rails—and how such an epiphany runs the risk of ridiculousness on the modern stage. In comparison with a divine prologue, the deus ex machina does have the advantage of the possibility of preparation, in the sense that the gods have already been discussed in the play, there is an established human frame against which divine difference can be sharply articulated, and a strong perception of the space of the action—the palace in this case—which can be used as a norm to define the god's transcendence.

Euripides' *Electra* shows this potential well. The play is set in and around the poor hut of the farmer to whom Electra has been married off. Clytemnestra is lured out of the palace in the city to the hut in the country, on the homely pretext of helping her daughter after the birth of a baby. She is killed there by the hesitant Orestes and the much more aggressive Electra. The two children are far from triumphant after the murder, and at that point the god Castor appears and delivers what is a remarkable speech even by Euripides' standards. He says that Orestes was wrong to do what he did; that Apollo was not wise in his oracles, but, because Apollo is his lord, he will say no more—a whitewash. Orestes should go to Athens, continues Castor, where he will be acquitted. The fact that Orestes has done wrong and yet will be acquitted with full divine authority is typical of Euripides' sardonic perspective on things. The gods take advantage of the shoddy business of show trials, just like humans. Castor's speech offers a strong formal closure to the action, and ties up the loose ends of who marries whom and who lives where ever after—but leaves the audience with perplexing uncertainty about the moral thrust of the whole.

Castor appears in the position of the god: he rises above and is set in contrast with the lowly hut, and with the humans in their shabby confusion and emotional despair. The play has talked already of the oracles of the gods and the worship of divinity and its place in a moral universe. The staging can capitalize on these contrasts and preparation in a way which the prologue of the *Trojan Women* cannot.

Some plays of Euripides have a divine epilogue, some a divine prologue, and *Hippolytus* has both—which more than doubles the problems for the director. It opens with Aphrodite, goddess of desire, and ends with an epiphany of Artemis, goddess of virginity and the hunt. A production has to deal both with the instantaneous entrance of the very embodiment of sexiness at the beginning of the play, and with the appearance of the chaste huntress who engages directly with the characters onstage at the end. These divine appearances frame intense and often violent human discussions of sexual desire and self-control. The balance between the human drama and the divine frame becomes a fundamental problem for any performance—and it is not surprising that modern adaptations, from Racine's *Phèdre* to Tony Harrison's *Phaedra Britannica*, have often cut the gods out entirely, which inevitably changes the dynamics of Euripides' play drastically.

Aphrodite [Venus] and Artemis [Diana], unlike Castor, are very familiar figures from Western art. This is both a resource and a difficulty. Both have an easy authority through such familiarity, and the structural parallel of their appearances at the beginning and end of the play reinforces that authority in dramatic terms. Yet their very familiarity also highlights the problem of costuming a god. Should a play follow any iconographic tradition—Artemis with her bow and hunting dress, Aphrodite naked or in revealing silks? Gods may be immortal but how should a "timeless" production dress a divinity? In a production with a modern mis-en-scène things are even murkier. A *Trojan Women* with a chorus of contemporary refugees—a common staging temptation, as we have seen—has first to face the issue of how a god can appear for the twenty-first century killing fields.

Where Aeschylus demands a world full of gods—a coherent and integrated representation of men, women, ghosts, monsters, divinities—and where Sophocles largely removes the gods as inscrutable powers behind the action of his tormented, excessive humans, Euripides tends to separate his divinities into the bounded space of the prologue or epilogue. This act of separation must always be the cue for the staging: the construction of a separate world of power, influence, certainty, control, beyond but constantly invading the messiness of the mundane human world. Such a separation raises a constant and insistent questioning for the audience about the competing forces and pressures that run (through) our lives. That is the challenge to the director, and the strength of Euripides' dramatic structuring: to embody that questioning in a physical staging.

]]] [[[

One play of Euripides, above all others, puts divinity center stage, with a god in its epilogue, in its prologue, and throughout the action too: the *Bacchae*. Dionysus opens the play with the announcement that he has arrived in human disguise and is determined to punish anyone who does not recognize him. That he is in human form and yet demands recognition as a god is the founding, paradoxical drive of this play—for the audience as well as the characters onstage. Do you understand? Can you *see* Dionysus's power? This is the question the *Bacchae* hurls at everyone. Dionysus is a god, but has a mortal mother. He comes from the East, but was born in Thebes. He is male, but dressed as a woman. He seems weak and unarmed, but eludes the power of kings. Dionysus embodies paradox. And demands recognition.[13] The action of the play dramatizes this provoking mix of slipperiness and injunction. The old men, Teiresias and Cadmus, dressed as women and ready to dance for the god—have they got the god right? Is their worship what is required? When Pentheus sees two suns and two cities, he is told by the god that now he is seeing what he should—like a proper celebrant of the mysteries of the god. Is Agave, mad dancer of the god, who pulls her son apart, doing the god's bidding—and at what cost?

The *Bacchae* tells us more about the physical appearance of Dionysus than we can learn about almost any other character in any ancient play. We know he has a smiling mask, that he has long black ringlets and pale skin, that he is effeminate to look at, young, delicate, and pretty, that he is garlanded, and wears a fawn skin. Yet the play asks us again and again whether we have truly seen and comprehended this paradoxical figure. Finally, the god appears in epiphany (though unfortunately a good chunk of this scene has not survived from the ancient world and has to be supplied or worked round for a modern performance). One of the most perplexing questions for a director is how Dionysus should appear in this final scene. Now he stands forth to proclaim his godhead. Is he still in disguise as a man, as a Bacchant, indeed? Or does he now appear in his full glory (however that is to be shown)? Or does he deliver the speech somehow unseen by the audience

in order to maintain the mystery? A choice here will funda-
mentally alter the view of Dionysus the play offers—but get
Dionysus wrong, says the play, and violent destruction is the
punishment.

Dionysus dominates the *Bacchae*. As a god, he gives the
prologue, which authoritatively says what the setting is and
what will unfurl; he gives the epilogue, where he lays down
the future for the human characters and proclaims his own divinity. In between, onstage he leads the human actors toward
their destruction, driving Agave to kill her son in a mocking
and horrific parody of a sacrifice to the god, and leading Pentheus toward humiliation and dismemberment. He directs,
stage-manages and stars in his own narrative. There is no
place outside Dionysus's story in theater, no place from which
we can get a bearing on the god of theater. Yet our percep-
tions are twisted by his world of illusion, and by his paradoxical demands to see what cannot be seen, and to comprehend
what does not fit into our categories of thought. In the *Bacchae*, how the gods are represented is a central theme of the
drama, as much as it is a production's challenge. The constant presence of the god onstage—the only example in Euripides—requires a quite different stagecraft from *Hippolytus*
or *Trojan Women*, say. The god creates and inhabits the world
in which the human beings live, and the whole play is enacted
under his smile.

The *Bacchae* is undoubtedly a masterpiece, but it has received surprisingly few modern professional productions, and
even fewer genuinely successful ones. (There have been hundreds of semiprofessional and amateur versions, however.) It
demands so much of a company in terms of staging, acting,
and conceptual grasp. Dionysus and his chorus of Bacchants
have particularly stimulated the imagination of directors.
In the National Theatre, London, in 1973, the Soyinka text
provoked a chorus and god inspired by African dance, seminaked, intensely rhythmic, and abandoned—and Dionysus

freed slaves to join the Bacchic chorus.[14] By contrast, the most recent production for the National Theatre by Sir Peter Hall was heavily stylized, masked, and gloriously dressed (and surprisingly lacking in emotion, especially in the final scenes).[15] Bafflingly, some of his Bacchants were bare-breasted, others not—as if there were an opt-out clause for wildness. In Schechner's *Dionysus in 69*, there was much nudity and writhing (a route many experimental companies have taken over the years), and an eventually discontinued attempt to involve the audience in the scenes of possession and release. The chorus of Bacchants inevitably frames the representation of the god, and all too many productions signally fail to capture the play's insistent threat of Dionysiac possession. One reviewer described Michael Cacoyannis's chorus at the Circle in the Square in New York in 1980 as "an ethically mixed group in sluttish costumes whose movements are rather like the floorshow in a medium-priced third-world bordello."[16] Liviu Ciulei's production at the Guthrie Theater in 1987 fared no better: "The ladies of the chorus did not appear to pose any discernable danger to the civil order of Thebes. They swirled their heavy gypsy skirts and shook their bangled arms at the balcony and declaimed their fortune cookies, but the effect was rather of a feminist rally than of women mad from Bacchus."[17] The power and threat of Dionysus can been played seminaked or in a business suit or in a fawn skin—but without a real sense of power and threat, the costuming is of little import.

]]] [[[

It is fitting that this book should end with the *Bacchae*, a play which embodies the richness of ancient theatrical resources as well as the power of ancient writing. Its status as a classic is unchallenged in the modern era. But it is also fitting that we end with Dionysus, the god of theater. Greek tragedy is the foundation and origin of Western theater—but that should not be a statement of pious historicism. It is the foundation of Western theater because of its continuing and constant influence on modern thought and practice, because its great plays continue to inspire remarkable performances, and because its power, its political and emotional provocations, and its profound explorations of the human condition continue to inspire, challenge, and fulfill artists and audiences. That's why staging Greek tragedy today still matters and why our theater is still under the sway of the smiling and dangerous Dionysus.

Notes

Introduction

1. Good starting points are F. Zeitlin, "The Body's Revenge: Dionysus and Tragic Action in Euripides' *Hecuba*," in her *Playing the Other* (Chicago, 1996); A. Michelini, *Euripides and the Tragic Tradition* (Madison and London, 1987), 131–80; J. Mossman, *Wild Justice* (Oxford, 1995); C. Segal, *Euripides and the Poetics of Sorrow* (Durham and London, 1993), 157–226; M. Nussbaum, *The Fragility of Goodness: Luck and Ethics in Greek Tragedy and Philosophy* (Cambridge, 1986), 397–421.

2. On staging see D. Wiles, *Tragedy in Athens: Performance Space and Theatrical Meaning* (Cambridge, 1997); D. Wiles, *Greek Theatre Performance: An Introduction* (Cambridge, 1990). O. Taplin's *Greek Tragedy in Action* (London, 1978) (which is an extension of his longer and more technical *The Stagecraft of Aeschylus* [Oxford, 1977]) has proven seminal in this field; E. Csapo and W. Slater, *The Context of Ancient Drama* (Ann Arbor, 1995). On the politics see J. Winkler and F. Zeitlin, eds., *Nothing to Do with Dionysus?* (Princeton, 1990); J.-P. Vernant and P. Vidal-Naquet, *Myth and Tragedy in Ancient Greece*, trans. J. Lloyd (Brighton, 1981); P. E. Easterling, ed., *The Cambridge Companion to Greek Tragedy* (Cambridge, 1997).

3. See in particular E. Hall and F. Macintosh, *Greek Tragedy and the British Theatre*,

1660–1914 (Oxford, 2005); E. Hall, F. Macintosh, and A. Wrigley, *Dionysus Since 69: Greek Tragedy at the Dawn of the Third Millennium* (Oxford, 2004); M. McDonald, *Ancient Sun, Modern Light: Greek Drama on the Modern Stage* (New York, 1992); M. McDonald and M. Walton, eds., *Amid Our Troubles: Irish Versions of Greek Tragedy* (London, 2002); K. Hartigan, *Greek Tragedy on the American Stage: Ancient Drama in the Commercial Theater, 1882–1994* (Westport, Conn., and London, 1995); the magnum opus of Helene Foley is eagerly awaited and promises to be the fullest treatment of Greek tragedy on the American stage. I have had my own go in *Who Needs Greek?* (Cambridge, 2002), 108–77.

4. The video libraries at the New York Public Library for the Performing Arts, Lincoln Center; at the Archive for the Performance of Greek and Roman Drama at Oxford; at the BBC, London, and of various friends, especially Helene Foley, were essential.

Chapter 1

1. For a good introduction to the problems of Greek theater space see D. Wiles, *Tragedy in Athens: Performance Space and Theatrical Meaning* (Cambridge, 1997), which has a useful brief bibliography of the long academic rows on this issue. His book is an extension of his own *Greek Theatre Performance: An Introduction* (Cambridge, 1990). O. Taplin's *Greek Tragedy in Action* (London, 1978) (which is an extension of his longer and more technical *The Stagecraft of Aeschylus* [Oxford, 1977]) has proven seminal in this field.

2. The scripts of *Les Atrides* include *Euripide: Iphigénie à Aulis*, trans. J. and M. Bollack (Théâtre du Soleil and Editions de Minuit, Paris, 1990); *Eschyle: L'Agamemnon*, trans. A. Mnouchkine (Théâtre du Soleil, Paris, 1990); *Les Choéphores* (Théâtre du Soleil, Paris, 1991); *Les Euménides*, trans. H. Cixous (Théâtre du Soleil, Paris, 1992). There are four CDs of music by Jean-Jacques Lemetre, and photographs published by Michèle Laurent also under the Théâtre du Soleil imprint. There is no commercially available video of the production. For a list of performances, cast, and reviews consult the database of the Archive of Performance of Greek and Roman Drama. The Théâtre du Soleil itself also has a useful Web site, www.lebacausoleil.com.

3. See S. Goldhill, *Reading Greek Tragedy* (Cambridge, 1986), 33–56; F. Zeitlin, "Dynamics of Misogyny in the *Oresteia*," in *Playing the Other* (Chicago, 1996).

4. Script: Lee Breuer: *The Gospel at Colonus* (New York, 1989). The cast recording of the 1985 Philadelphia production is widely available. A decent video of the production can be seen at the Lincoln Center Library of Performing Arts.

5. This opened at the Abbey Theatre in June 2000, and the production used the K. McLeish and F. Raphael translation of *Medea* (London, 1994).

6. Opened 10 September 1992 at the Almeida Theatre London. The production used the A. Elliot translation (London, 1993).

7. The production used the ancient Greek text. Materials from the production can be consulted in the archive of the Cambridge Greek Play in the University Library, Cambridge.

8. The production of Deborah Warner starring Fiona Shaw actually premiered at the Pit, at the Royal Shakespeare's London residence of the Barbican in 1988, but was also produced in the early 1990s in London. David Leveaux directed Zoë Wanamaker at the Donmar Theatre in London, in 1997. Neil Sissons directed Jane Montgomery for the Compass Theatre Company, which toured several cities in England. Andrei Serban brought his production to the Edinburgh Festival in 1992. Also in 1990 Friedrich Götz produced Strauss's *Electra* at Covent Garden in a celebrated performance.

9. For a performance history of the Strauss production see S. Goldhill, *Who Needs Greek?* (Cambridge, 2002), 108–77.

10. See P. Easterling, "The Early Years of the Cambridge Greek Play: 1882–1912," in C. Stray, ed., *Classics in 19th and 20th Century Cambridge: Curriculum, Culture, and Community* (*PCPS* Supplement 24, Cambridge, 1998).

11. See E. Hall, F. Macintosh, and A. Wrigley, eds., *Dionysus Since 69: Greek Tragedy at the Dawn of the Third Millennium* (Oxford, 2004), especially the chapter in it by F. Zeitlin entitled "Dionysus in 69." The Archive of Performance of Greek and Roman Drama lists 144 productions between 1970 and 1999.

Chapter 2

1. See P. Wilson, "The *Aulos* in Athens" and E. Hall, "Actor's Song in Tragedy," both in S. Goldhill and R. Osborne, eds., *Performance Culture and Athenian Democracy* (Cambridge, 1999).

2. On the chorus, see the chapters of J. Gould and S. Goldhill in M. Silk, ed., *Tragedy and the Tragic: Greek Theatre and Beyond* (Oxford, 1996). See also Albert Henrichs, "'Why Should I Dance?' Choral Self-Referentiality in Greek Tragedy," *Arion* 3 (1994–95): 56–111; and P. Wilson, "Leading the Tragic *Khoros*: Tragic Prestige in the Democratic City," in C. Pelling, ed., *Greek Tragedy and the Historian* (Oxford, 1997).

3. On the hero see Bernard Knox, *The Heroic Temper: Studies in Sophoclean Tragedy* (Berkeley, 1964); R. Winnington-Ingram, *Sophocles: An Interpretation* (Cambridge, 1980), 304ff; S. Goldhill, *Reading Greek Tragedy* (Cambridge, 1986), 138–67.

4. See Claude Calame, *Choruses of Young Women in Ancient Greece*, trans. D. Collins and J. Orion (Lanham, Md., 1997).

5. See J. Winkler and F. Zeitlin, eds., *Nothing to Do with Dionysus? Athenian Drama in Its Social Context* (Princeton, 1990); M. Silk, ed., *Tragedy and the Tragic* (Oxford, 1996); P. Easterling, ed. *The Cambridge Companion to Greek Tragedy* (Cambridge, 1997).

6. The quotation is from Thucydides' celebrated version of Pericles' Funeral Speech over the War Dead (book 2 of Thucydides, chapters 34–46), exhaustively but excellently analyzed by Nicole Loraux in *The Invention of Athens*, trans. A. Sheridan (Cambridge, Mass., 1986). See also M. Finley, *Politics in the Ancient World* (Cambridge, 1983).

7. See the chapters of J. Gould and S. Goldhill in M. Silk, ed., *Tragedy and the Tragic* (Oxford, 1996), which debate the importance of the chorus's marginal social status in particular.

8. Mitchell's production opened at the National Theatre in London in June 2004. The translation was by D. Taylor (*Euripides: Plays*, trans. P. Arnott, D. Taylor, and M. Walton, with an introduction by M. Walton [London 1991]). Mitchell had produced the *Iphigeneia at Aulis* in 2001 at the Abbey Theatre at Dublin, also with Kate Duchene as Clytemnestra.

9. B. Picon-Vallin, "L'Orient au Théâtre du Soleil: Le pays imaginaire, les sources concrètes, le travail original (rencontre avec Ariane Mnouchkine et Hélène Cixous)," which can be consulted

on the Web site of Théâtre du Soleil, www.lebacausoleil.com. My translation.

10. For an introduction to Kathakali, see P. Zarrilli, *Kathakali Dance-Drama: Where Gods and Demons Come to Play* (London and New York, 2000).

11. The phrase is taken from A. Neuschäfer, *De l'improvisation au rite, l'épopée de notre temps: Le Théâtre du Soleil au carrefour des genres* (Frankfurt-am-Rein, 2002).

12. Mnouchkine talks repeatedly about the Orient in interviews. See A. Kiernander, *Ariane Mnouchkine and the Théâtre du Soleil* (Cambridge, 1993); D. Williams, *Collaborative Theatre: The Théâtre du Soleil Sourcebook* (London, 1999). Her remarks always go back to Antonin Artaud's comment "The theatre is Oriental."

13. See S. Goldhill, *Reading Greek Tragedy* (Cambridge, 1986), chapter 3.

14. The production opened at the National Theatre, London, in November 1981. Script: T. Harrison, *The Oresteia* (London, 1981); music, Harrison Birtwistle.

15. Harrison writes in the published script, "This text is written to be performed, a rhythmic libretto for masks, music, and an all-male company."

16. See O. Taplin, "Masks in Greek Tragedy and in *Tantalus*," *Didaskalia* 2 (2001); also D. Wiles, "The Use of Masks in Modern Performances of Greek Drama," in E. Hall, F. Macintosh, and A. Wrigley, *Dionysus Since 69* (Oxford, 2004). Wiles's thoughts on the ancient mask are fully discussed in *The Masks of Menander* (Cambridge, 1991).

17. The ten plays are published in J. Barton, *Tantalus* (London, 2000), though this script was not the performance script. There is a very useful discussion of *Tantalus* in *Didaskalia* 2 (2001). Ben Phelan and Dirk Olson made a documentary entitled *Tantalus: Behind the Mask*, which recorded the preparations for the first production in Denver.

18. See J. Montgomery, "*Tantalus* and the Problem of the Chorus," *Didaskalia* 2 (2001).

19. The production opened in Chichester before transferring to the Donmar in October 1997 (before playing at Princeton and then in New York). It used the Frank McGuinness translation (*Sophocles' Electra* [New York, 1997]). Leveaux had previously directed a Japanese translation of the Hugo von Hofmannsthal version of *Electra* in Tokyo in 1996.

20. The script was by F. McGuinness (*Euripides' Hecuba in a New Version* [London 2002]), and the show opened in September 2004.

21. See R. Padel, "Imagery of Elsewhere: Two Choral Odes of Euripides," *Classical Quarterly* 24 (1974): 227–41.

22. Script: T. Harrison, *Euripides' Hecuba* (London, 2005). The show opened at the Alberry Theatre, London, in April 2005 (company, Royal Shakespeare Company), before transferring to Washington, New York, and then Greece.

23. The show opened October 1995 in the Other Place Stratford before transferring to the Royal Shakespeare's London residence at the Barbican. It used the D. Thompson translation (*Euripides: Plays 1* [London, 2000], translated by M. Walton and D. Thompson, with an introduction by M. Walton). David Thompson had directed his own production of the play, under the title *The Sons of Oedipus*, at the Greenwich Theatre in London in 1977.

24. See E. Hall and F. Macintosh, *Greek Tragedy and the British Theatre, 1660–1914* (Oxford, 2005), 508–10. This book is an indispensable source for the history of British theater's response to tragedy.

25. The best general study of the play is N. Croally's *Euripidean Polemic: The Trojan Women and the Function of Tragedy* (Cambridge, 1994).

26. On the *Oresteia* see S. Goldhill, *Aeschylus: The Oresteia* (Cambridge, 2004).

27. See F. Zeitlin, "The Argive Festival of Hera and Euripides' *Electra*," *Transactions and Proceedings of the American Philological Association* 101 (1970): 645–69; S. Goldhill, *Reading Greek Tragedy* (Cambridge, 1986), 245–59.

Chapter 3

1. Personal conversation, October 2005.

2. On the physical side of Hecuba's role, see F. Zeitlin, "The Body's Revenge: Dionysus and Tragic Action in Euripides' *Hecuba*," in *Playing the Other* (Chicago, 1996); in general, also, A. Michelini, *Euripides and the Tragic Tradition* (Madison and London, 1987), 131–80; J. Mossman, *Wild Justice* (Oxford, 1995), though her views on the erotics of the death of Polyxena are odd; C. Segal, *Euripides and the Poetics of Sorrow* (Durham and London, 1993), 157–226.

3. *Didaskalia* 3 (2002), in the panel discussion chaired by Adrian Poole.

4. I have discussed the politics of this line at greater length in "Antigone and the Politics of Sisterhood," in V. Zajko and M. Leonard, eds., *Laughing with Medusa: Classical Myth and Feminist Thought* (Oxford, 2006).

5. For the Polus story see Aulus Gellius 6.5. On Greek and Roman actors see P. Easterling and E. Hall, eds., *Greek and Roman Actors: Aspects of an Ancient Profession* (Cambridge, 2002).

6. The first production, directed by Bob Crowley and Stephen Rea, opened in October 1990 at the Guildhall in Derry, Northern Ireland, before transferring to the Tricycle Theatre, London. Script: S. Heaney, *The Cure at Troy: A Version of Sophocles' Philoctetes* (London, 1990). Recent American productions: 1993, directed by Derek Walcott in New York; 1995, directed by Tony Taccone at the Oregon Shakespeare Festival; 1996, the American Repertory Theatre at Cambridge, Mass., directed by Leland Paton; 1998, by the Yale Repertory Company, New Haven, directed by Liz Diamond; 2002, at the Blue Heron Theatre, New York, directed by Kevin Osborne.

7. Discussed at length by C. Segal in *Tragedy and Civilization* (Cambridge, Mass., 1981), 328–61.

8. See O. Taplin, *Greek Tragedy in Action* (London, 1978), 76–100.

9. *The Oresteia* opened in December 1999 at the National Theatre in London, and also played in Toronto in 2000 at the du Maurier World Stage Festival. The script: Ted Hughes, *The Oresteia: A New Version* (London, 1999).

10. The story of Timotheus comes from the scholion (an ancient marginal comment) on Sophocles *Ajax* 864.

11. Peter Stein's production opened in the Schaubühne am Halleschen Ufer in Berlin in 1980, and played Paris (Maison de la Culture Bobigny) in 1981 and Ostia (Rome) in 1984. It was revived and redirected in Russian in Moscow in 1994, from where it went to Epidaurus in Greece, and then the Edinburgh International Festival. Script for the German production: P. Stein, *Die Orestie des Aischylos* (Munich, 1977). A video of the German production is consultable at the Archive of Performance of Greek and Roman Drama in Oxford.

12. See Silvia Montiglio, *Silence in the Land of Logos* (Princeton, 2000), for a good discussion of silence in Greek culture.

13. See S. Goldhill, "The Language of Tragedy: Rhetoric and Communication," in P. Easterling, ed., *The Cambridge Companion to Greek Tragedy* (Cambridge, 1997).

14. See B. Knox, "The *Hippolytus* of Euripides," *Yale Classical Studies* 13 (1952): 1–31, reprinted in B. Knox, *Word and Action* (Baltimore and London, 1979).

15. See S. Goldhill, *Reading Greek Tragedy* (Cambridge, 1986), 57–78.

16. Interview with Nicole Plett, *US 1 Newspaper*, 16 September 1998.

17. See C. Pelling, ed., *Characterization and Individuality in Greek Literature* (Oxford, 1990).

18. E. Fraenkel, *Aeschylus: Agamemnon* (Oxford, 1950), 2:441–42; J. Denniston and D. Page, *Aeschylus: Agamemnon* (Oxford, 1957), 151–52.

19. See R. Winnington-Ingram, *Sophocles: An Interpretation* (Cambridge, 1980). The internalization of the Furies is central to Hofmannsthal's Electra, and the whole twentieth-century reading of the play: see S. Goldhill, *Who Needs Greek?* (Cambridge, 2002), 108–77.

20. Interview with Nicole Plett, *US 1 Newspaper*, 16 September 1998.

21. From an interview with Richard Covington in *Salon*, 11 April 6–21, 1996.

Chapter 4

1. For the *Electras* see above, chapter 1, note 8. *Ion*: 1994, Royal Shakespeare Company at the Barbican in London, using the David Lan adaptation (*Ion/Euripides* [London, 1994]), directed by Nicholas Wright and starring Jude Law; 1994, Lyric Theatre, Hammersmith, London, directed by Nick Philippou, using a Kenneth McLeish translation (apparently unpublished); 2002, Gate, Notting Hill, London, directed by Erica Whyman, using a translation by Stephen Sharkey (unpublished); 2003, an opera composed by Param Vir, at the Royal Opera House, Covent Garden (and elsewhere in Europe and Britain), based on the David Lan adaptation; 2004, Mercury Theatre Company, Colchester, using a translation by M. Poulter (unpublished), directed by David Hunt.

2. *New York Review of Books*, 13 February 2003, 24–29, by Daniel Mendelsohn, who has, it should be noted, also written a book which focuses on the play: *Gender and the City in Euripides' Political Plays* (Oxford, 2002).

3. Quoted by Zoë Wanamaker in an interview with Nicole Plett in *US 1 Newspaper*, 16 September 1998.

4. See P. Easterling, *The Cambridge Companion to Greek Tragedy* (Cambridge, 1997), especially 3–68.

5. For the audience of Greek tragedy see S. Goldhill, "The Audience of Greek Tragedy," in P. Easterling, *The Cambridge Companion to Greek Tragedy* (Cambridge, 1997).

6. See S. Goldhill, "The Great Dionysia and Civic Ideology," in J. Winkler and F. Zeitlin, *Nothing to Do with Dionysus?* (Princeton, 1990).

7. See F. Zeitlin, "Playing the Other: Theater, Theatricality, and the Feminine in Greek Drama," in her *Playing the Other* (Chicago, 1996).

8. The story is printed in F. Dunn, ed., *Sophocles' Electra in Performance* (Stuttgart, 1996).

9. Directed by Annie Castledine at the National Theatre and using the K. McLeish translation (*Women of Troy* [London, 2004]).

10. See F. Turner, *The Greek Heritage in Victorian Britain* (New Haven, 1981); E. Butler, *The Tyranny of Greece over the German Imagination* (Cambridge, 1935).

11. In her interview with Nicole Plett, *US 1 Newspaper*, 16 September 1998.

12. Frank McGuiness, the translator, says that the greatcoat is "a reflection of her own psychic and sexual disturbance, confusion"; Joseph Long, "The Sophoclean Killing Fields: An Interview with Frank McGuinness," in M. McDonald and M. Walton, eds., *Amid Our Troubles: Irish Versions of Greek Tragedy* (London, 2002).

13. Matthews's *Antigone* is not published. Brendan Kennelly, *Sophocles' Antigone: A New Version* (Newcastle-upon-Tyne, 1996); and Tom Paulin's *The Riot Act: A Version of Sophocles' Antigone* (London, 1985) are the other two written that year. Athol Fugard's *The Island* was also produced that year in Ireland.

14. National Theatre Education Workpack, on *The Oresteia*. A video of the production can be consulted at the National Theatre archive.

15. Ibid.

16. Charles Spencer, *Daily Telegraph*, 3 December 1999.

17. M. Billington, *Guardian*, 3 December 1999.

18. In an interview with Gideon Lester for *ARTicles* 1.2 (December 2002), an online journal for the American Repertory Theatre.

19. Robert Auletta, *The Persians: Aeschylus* (Los Angeles, 1993).

20. The story is told in Herodotus *Histories* 6.18–21.

21. See Katie Fleming, "Fascism on Stage: Jean Anouilh's *Antigone*," in V. Zajko and M. Leonard, eds., *Laughing with Medusa: Classical Myth and Feminist Thought* (Oxford, 2006).

22. For the background to this, see Athol Fugard, "*Antigone* in Africa," in M. McDonald and M. Walton, eds., *Amid Our Troubles: Irish Versions of Greek Tragedy* (London, 2002).

23. Ibid. For the script see Athol Fugard, *Township Plays* (Oxford, 1999).

24. See S. Goldhill, *Reading Greek Tragedy* (Cambridge, 1986), 79–106; M. Whitlock Blundell, *Helping Friends and Harming Enemies* (Cambridge, 1989), 106–48.

25. See George Steiner, *Antigones* (Oxford, 1984).

26. See Tom Paulin, "Antigone," in M. McDonald and M. Walton, eds., *Amid Our Troubles: Irish Versions of Greek Tragedy* (London, 2002).

27. In M. McDonald and M. Walton, eds., *Amid Our Troubles: Irish Versions of Greek Tragedy* (London, 2002), 167.

28. Tom Paulin, "Antigone," in M. McDonald and M. Walton, eds., *Amid Our Troubles: Irish Versions of Greek Tragedy* (London, 2002), 167–68. See also Seamus Deane, "Field Day's Greeks (and Russians)," in M. McDonald and M. Walton, eds., *Amid Our Troubles: Irish Versions of Greek Tragedy* (London, 2002), 153–56.

29. See E. Hall and F. Macintosh, *Greek Tragedy and the British Theatre, 1660–1914* (Oxford, 2005), 391–421.

30. See Nicole Loraux, *Tragic Ways to Kill a Woman*, trans. A. Forster (Cambridge, Mass. 1987); F. Zeitlin, *Playing the Other* (Chicago, 1996); Helene Foley, *Female Acts in Greek Tragedy* (Princeton, 2001); Victoria Wohl, *Intimate Commerce: Exchange, Gender, and Subjectivity in Greek Tragedy* (Austin, 1998); Laura McClure, *Spoken Like a Woman: Speech and Gender in Athenian Drama* (Princeton, 1999).

31. Seamus Heaney, "*The Cure at Troy* Production Notes in No Particular Order," in M. McDonald and M. Walton, eds., *Amid Our Troubles: Irish Versions of Greek Tragedy* (London, 2002). Clinton wrote a book called *Between History and Hope: America's Challenge for the 21st Century* (New York, 1997), a title which also seems to echo Heaney's lines.

Chapter 5

1. V. Nabokov, *Poems and Problems* (New York, 1970), 175.
2. Translations: R. Gibbons, *Bakkhai: Euripides* (Oxford, 2001); D. Franklin, *Euripides: Bacchae* (Cambridge, 2000); D. Slavitt and P. Bovie, *Euripides 1* (Philadelphia, 1998); J. Morwood, *Euripides: Iphigeneia among the Taurians; Bacchae; Iphigeneia at Aulis; Rhesus* (Oxford, 1999); P. Woodruff, *Euripides: Bacchae* (Indianapolis/ Cambridge, 1988); P. Vellacott, *Euripides: Bacchae and Other Plays* (Harmondsworth, 1954).
3. F. Raphael and K. McLeish, *Bacchae by Euripides* (London, 1998).
4. H. Lloyd-Jones, *Aeschylus: Oresteia: Agamemnon* (London, 1979).
5. F. Raphael and K. McLeish, *The Serpent Son: Aeschylus' Oresteia* (Cambridge, 1979).
6. *New York Times*, 29 November 1998, 7.
7. Including Declan Donnelly's *Philoctetes* in 1988; Warner's *Electra* in 1988; Boswell's *Hecuba* at the Gate, Notting Hill, in 1992; *The Clytemnestra Project* at the Guthrie Theater, Minneapolis (Garland Wright); *The Women of Troy* at the National Theatre, London, in 1995 (Annie Castledine); Warner's *Medea* in 2000.
8. T. Harrison, *Aeschylus: The Oresteia* (London, 1981).
9. T. Hughes, *Aeschylus: The Oresteia* (London, 1999).
10. P. Meineck, *Aeschylus: Oresteia* (Indianapolis and Cambridge, 1998), xlviii.
11. B. Kennelly, *Euripides' Medea: A New Version* (Newcastle-upon-Tyne, 1991); *Euripides' The Trojan Women: A New Version* (Newcastle-upon-Tyne, 2003); *Sophocles' Antigone: A New Version* (Newcastle-upon-Tyne, 1993).
12. It was originally commissioned as a libretto by the Metropolitan Opera in New York, but the composer died before it was finished. It was produced by the Volcano Theatre Company from Wales under the director Janek Alexander, and was performed at the ICA (Institute for Contemporary Art) in London in May 1991. The script is published in T. Harrison, *Theatre Works, 1973–85* (Harmondsworth, 1985).
13. This and the following quotations come from Kennelly's piece in M. McDonald and M. Walton, eds., *Amid Our Troubles: Irish Versions of Greek Tragedy* (London, 2002).
14. A. Elliot, *Medea/Euripides* (London, 1993).

15. F. Raphael and K. McLeish, *Medea by Euripides* (London, 1994).

16. T. Paulin, "Antigone," in M. McDonald and M. Walton, eds., *Amid Our Troubles: Irish Versions of Greek Tragedy* (London, 2002), 168–69.

17. Ibid., 165.

18. *The Thebans* opened in Stratford in 1991 and transferred to the Barbican in London. Script: T. Wertenbaker, *The Thebans: Oedipus Tyrannus, Oedipus at Colonus, and Antigone* (London, 1992); subsequently *Oedipus Tyrannus, Oedipus at Kolonos, and Antigone/Sophocles* (London, 1997).

19. K. McLeish, *Electra, Antigone, Philoctetes/Sophocles* (Cambridge, 1979).

20. S. Heaney, *Burial at Thebes: Sophocles' Antigone* (London, 2004).

21. *Collected Poems of W. B. Yeats*, ed. R. Finnegan (New York, 1996), 276.

22. F. McGuinness, *Electra/Sophocles* (London, 1997).

23. T. Hughes, *Aeschylus: The Oresteia* (London, 1999); T. Harrison, *Aeschylus: The Oresteia* (London, 1981); R. Fagles, *Aeschylus: The Oresteia* (New York, 1966); R. Lowell, *The Oresteia of Aeschylus* (London, 1979); P. Meineck, *Aeschylus: Oresteia* (Indianapolis and Cambridge, 1998); A. Shapiro and P. Burian, *The Oresteia/Aeschylus* (Oxford, 2003).

24. T. Wertenbaker, *The Thebans: Oedipus Tyrannus, Oedipus at Colonus and Antigone* (London, 1992); D. Taylor, *Sophocles 1: The Theban Plays* (London, 1993); K. McLeish, *Electra, Antigone, Philoctetes/Sophocles* (Cambridge, 1979); F. McGuinness, *Electra/Sophocles* (London, 1997); R. Grene and R. Lattimore, *The Complete Greek Tragedies* (Chicago, 1956); E. F. Watling, *Theban Plays* (Harmondsworth, 1969); S. Heaney, *Burial at Thebes: Sophocles Antigone* (London, 2004); *The Cure at Troy: A Version of Sophocles' Philoctetes* (London, 1990); Sir Richard Jebb, *Sophocles*, 7 vols. (Cambridge, 1883–98).

25. See F. Zeitlin, "Dionysus in 69," in E. Hall, F. Macintosh, and A. Wrigley, eds., *Dionysus Since 69* (Oxford, 2004); E. Hall, F. Macintosh and O. Taplin, eds., *Medea in Performance, 1500–2000* (Oxford, 2000); M. McDonald, "Medea as Politician and Diva: Riding the Dragon into the Future," in J. Clauss and S. Iles Johnston, eds., *Medea* (Princeton, 1997).

26. D. Rudkin, *Hippolytus/Euripides* (London, 1980)—produced by the Royal Shakespeare Company at the Other Place, Stratford, in 1978

with Juliet Stevenson as Aphrodite and Artemis, and Michael Pennington as Hippolytus, directed by Ron Daniel; A. Elliot, *Medea/ Euripides* (London, 1993); F. Raphael and K. McLeish, *Medea by Euripides* (London, 1994); F. McGuinness, *Euripides' Hecuba* (London, 2004); T. Wertenbaker, *Hecuba by Euripides* (Woodstock, London, Melbourne, 1996); K. McLeish, *After the Trojan War: Women of Troy, Hecuba, Helen* (London, 1996); F. Raphael and K. McLeish, *Bacchae by Euripides* (London, 1998).

27. Charles Mee's *Big Love* is a reworking of Aeschylus's *Suppliant Maidens*; see also his *Trojan Women: A Love Story*; Robert Auletta has scripted *The Persians* (Los Angeles, 1994) and *Ajax*, both directed by Peter Sellars, and the *Oresteia* for the American Repertory Theatre; Brendan Kennelly, *Medea* (Newcastle-upon-Tyne, 1991); *Trojan Women* (Newcastle-upon-Tyne, 1993); *Sophocles' Antigone* (Newcastle-upon-Tyne, 1996).

Chapter 6

1. P. Meineck, *Aeschylus: Oresteia* (Indianapolis and Cambridge, 1998).

2. *Vita Aesch* 9; Pollux 4.110.

3. T. Hughes, *Alcestis: Euripides* (London 1999).

4. On Hercules, see A. Blanchard, *Hercules: Scenes from a Heroic Life* (London, 2005).

5. This scene is discussed in N. Croally, *Euripidean Polemic* (Cambridge, 1994), 134–62; S. Goldhill, *Reading Greek Tragedy* (Cambridge, 1986), 234–38.

6. Annie Castledine at the National Theatre in London, 1995; Jane Montgomery at the Cambridge Arts Theatre in 1998.

7. R. Barthes, *S/Z*, tran. R. Miller (London, 1975), 33–34.

8. For the importance of Homer on tragedy, se S. Goldhill, *Reading Greek Tragedy* (Cambridge, 1986), 138–67.

9. Herodotus *Histories* 2.53.

10. S. Heaney, "*The Cure at Troy:* Production Notes in No Particular Order," in M. McDonald and M. Walton, eds., *Amid Our Troubles: Irish Versions of Greek Tragedy* (London, 2002), 172.

11. G. Steiner, *Antigones* (Oxford, 1984).

12. S. Heaney, *Burial at Thebes: Sophocles' Antigone* (London, 2004).

13. See H. Foley, "The Masque of Dionysus," *Transactions and Proceedings of the American Philological Association* 110 (1980): 107–33; S. Goldhill, *Reading Greek Tragedy* (Cambridge, 1986), 265–86.

14. W. Soyinka, *The Bacchae of Euripides* (London, 1973), subtitled "A Communion Rite."

15. National Theatre, 2002, with music by Harrison Birtwistle, who also composed the music for the Harrison/Hall *Oresteia*; translation by Colin Teevan; Dionysus was played by Greg Hicks, who had played Orestes in the *Oresteia* (and starred in *Tantalus*).

16. J. Simpson, *New York*, 20 October 1980.

17. T. Disch, *The Nation*, 12 September 1987.

Further Reading

A bibliography on Greek tragedy could contain thousands of items. This list offers some highly recommended books and articles. Each has further bibliography; there are other suggestions in the footnotes above.

Performance

Taplin, O. *Greek Tragedy in Action.* London, 1978.

Wiles, D. *Tragedy in Athens: Performance Space and Theatrical Meaning.* Cambridge, 1997.

History of Performance: General

Hall, E., and F. Macintosh. *Greek Tragedy and the British Theatre, 1660–1914.* Oxford, 2005.

Hall, E., F. Macintosh, and A. Wrigley. *Dionysus Since 69: Greek Tragedy at the Dawn of the Third Millennium.* Oxford, 2004.

McDonald, M., and M. Walton, eds. *Amid Our Troubles: Irish Versions of Greek Tragedy.* London, 2002.

History of Performance: Some Individual Plays

Goldhill, S. "Blood from the Shadows: Strauss' Disgusting, Degenerate *Elektra*." In *Who Needs Greek? Contests in the Cultural History of Hellenism.* Cambridge 2002.

Hall, E., F. Macintosh, and O. Taplin, eds. *Medea in Performance*. Oxford, 2000.

Macintosh, F., P. Michelakis, E. Hall, and O. Taplin, eds. *Agamemnon in Performance, 458 BC to AD 2004*. Oxford, 2005.

Context of Tragedy

Easterling, P. E., ed. *The Cambridge Companion to Greek Tragedy*. Cambridge, 1997.

Winkler, J., and F. Zeitlin, eds. *Nothing to Do with Dionysus?* Princeton, 1990.

Criticism of Greek Tragedy

Goldhill, S. *Aeschylus: The Oresteia*. Cambridge, 2004.

Goldhill, S. *Reading Greek Tragedy*. Cambridge, 1986.

Knox, B. *Word and Action*. Baltimore, 1979.

Segal, C. P. *Tragedy and Civilization: An Interpretation on Sophocles*. Cambridge, Mass., 1982.

Silk, M. S. *Tragedy and the Tragic: Greek Theatre and Beyond*. Oxford, 1996.

Vernant, J. P., and P. Vidal-Naquet. *Myth and Tragedy in Ancient Greece*. Trans. J. Lloyd. Brighton, 1981.

Winnington-Ingram, R. *Sophocles: An Interpretation*. Cambridge, 1980.

Tragedy and Gender

Foley, H. *Female Acts in Greek Tragedy*. Princeton, 2001.

Zeitlin, F. *Playing the Other*. Chicago, 1996.

Figure credits

3, 9, 16. Photos by Martine Franck, courtesy Magnum Photos.

4. Attributed to the Policoro Painter (South Italy, active 420–380 BC). *Lucanian Calyx-Krater*, c. 400 BC. Red-figure earthenware with added white, red, yellow, and brown wash; H. 50.5 cm. © The Cleveland Museum of Art, Leonard C. Hanna, Jr., Fund 1991.1.

5. Stephanie Berger, © 2006. Copyright belongs to Stephanie Berger. All rights reserved.

6, 7. Photos © Ben Payne.

8. Clarence Fountain and The Blind Boys of Alabama in *The Gospel at Colonus* from the Goodman Theatre's production. Photo: Liz Lauren.

10. Photo by Ivan Kyncl.

11. Photo courtesy Ruth Walz.

12. Photo courtesy Rulphin Coudyzer.

13. Museo Archeologico Nazionale, Naples, Italy.

14. Adolphe William Bouguereau (French, 1825–1905). *Orestes Pursued by the Furies*, 1862. Oil on canvas, 91 × 109 ⅝ inches. Chrysler Museum of Art, Norfolk, VA, Gift of Walter P. Chrysler, Jr., 71.623.

15. American Repertory Theatre production of *The Oresteia*, directed by François Rochaix, November 1994. Will LeBow, Randy Danson, Karen Phillips, Starla Benford, Sherri Parker Lee, in *The Eumenides*.

17. Archive of the Royal National Theatre, London. Photo by Nobby Clark.
18. Photo by Ruth Walz, courtesy of the Archive of Performances of Greek and Roman Drama, Oxford, UK.
19. *Hercules Farnese.* Museo Archeologico Nazionale, Naples, Italy. Photo courtesy Alinari/Art Resource, NY.
20. American Repertory Theatre production of *The Oresteia*, directed by François Rochaix, November 1994.

Index